THE REFERENCE SHELF

HUMAN LIFE:

Controversies and Concerns

edited by BRUCE BOHLE

THE REFERENCE SHELF
Volume 51 Number 5

THE H. W. WILSON COMPANY
New York 1979

THE REFERENCE SHELF

The books in this series contain reprints of articles, excerpts from books, and addresses on current issues and social trends in the United States and other countries. There are six separately bound numbers in each volume, all of which are generally published in the same calendar year. One number is a collection of recent speeches; each of the others is devoted to a single subject and gives background information and discussion from various points of view, concluding with a comprehensive bibliography. Books in the series may be purchased individually or on subscription.

Library of Congress Cataloging in Publication Data

Main entry under title:

Human life.

   (The Reference shelf; v. 51, no. 5)
   Bibliography: p.
   1. Bioethics—Addresses, essays, lectures.
2. Medical ethics—Addresses, essays, lectures.
I. Bohle, Bruce. II. Series: Reference shelf
v. 51, no. 5.
QH332.H85   174'.2   79-23453
ISBN 0-8242-0635-5

PRINTED IN THE UNITED STATES OF AMERICA

PREFACE

For as long as it has been part of our language, the phrase "a matter of life and death" has commanded instant attention. In the period ushered in by the 1970s, moreover, the words have taken on even greater urgency. This book is a reflection of that added significance. It deals with a wide range of matters of human life and death—with abortion, artificial insemination and fertilization, euthanasia, suicide, the use of scarce medical resources, experimentation on human subjects, psychosurgery, organ transplants, and the area of research known as genetic engineering.

The perspective of this book is not clinical but ethical and humane. It is not confined to scientific abstraction but focused on the application of science and medicine to ordinary life in today's world. This is a period that began with concern over countercultures, school integration, student unrest, and Vietnam. The country has been immersed in the crisis of Watergate and matters of ecology, energy, and inflation, as well as the intertwined issues of feminism and human rights—issues with which many of the subjects of this book are directly related. No less perplexing than our other troubles, the moral questions raised by the direct impact of technology upon individual lives continue to vex us.

A good gauge of the importance of a subject is the amount of new terminology that it inspires. Language is a reflection of its time. Events of the turbulent 1960s brought *dropout, psychedelic, busing, "Uncle Tom,"* and *teach-in* into our vocabularies. More recently, we have come across, with increasing frequency, expressions such as *man playing God, right to life* and *right to die* (or *death with dignity*), *pulling the plug* (of a life-sustaining machine), *living will, informed consent, triage, gene splicing, genetic screening, recombinant DNA, fertilization* in vitro, and *cloning.*

5

Each of the terms in this second group is defined and widely illustrated in the pages ahead, as is *bioethics,* the key to the theme of the book: ethical considerations pertaining to the life (biological) sciences. The new biology has brought many *biohazards,* and one of its pursuits is *bioengineering,* which deals in part with the creation of artificial organs and other internal body parts. Even *life* and *death* have been defined and redefined. They are very old terms, but exact definitions are now more crucial than ever. Precisely when does human life begin, and end?

Significantly, only part of this spate of new language is purely scientific in tone. Much of it has a distinctively ethical flavor; we have misgivings about scientific advances that may not, after all, be "good" in the moral or religious sense. But the gap separating belief from so-called pure science is not new. Earlier in human history, life and death tended to be regarded as something not only beyond our control but beyond our proper investigation. To cite one example, when inoculation for smallpox was introduced in Europe early in the eighteenth century, it was resisted as "unnatural and even impious." In Boston in 1721, as a smallpox epidemic took a toll of 850 lives, the pioneer physician Zabdiel Boylston, who led the drive for inoculation, was pilloried in the local press. Boylston's house was attacked, and he is said to have used a disguise in making his rounds.

Smallpox is a disease now virtually extinct. Yet in February 1979 there occurred in England an accident that could have caused a new epidemic—the escape of a smallpox virus from a laboratory at the University of Birmingham. But the accident raised a much larger bioethical issue: Should stocks of such a deadly virus be kept at all, even for research purposes? Concerns that are almost identical have been expressed over a much newer branch of research—experimentation with DNA, the tool of genetic engineering. Nor are these fears based on isolated occurrences; though even an isolated case of technological disaster is cause for alarm, so high have the stakes risen. And with the nuclear reactor accident at Three Mile Island, Pennsylvania, in March 1979, the mood of the entire nation changed perceptibly.

The eighteenth century conflict over smallpox inoculations seems an ancient battle between superstition and enlightenment. No longer is such medical intervention held to be in an area beyond proper human concern. Other questions, however—not all arising from innovative techniques—continue to generate controversy, and concerned lay citizens join forces to support or oppose concerned practitioners in order to effect regulation of the biological sciences.

In the United States, as in most other technically advanced countries, work in genetic engineering, psychosurgery (which entails cutting of the human brain), and *in vitro* fertilization (the process used in the birth of "test-tube" babies) is under special governmental control. Though it is often stated that abortion was legalized in the United States in 1973, the legalizing was subject to quite definite restrictions. And the work of national and state legislators since that time, with respect to public funding of such operations, has been even more restrictive.

The well-publicized case of Karen Ann Quinlan, a young New Jersey woman who became comatose in 1975 and continued to survive in a nursing home after a lengthy court battle over removal of her life-support system, did much to focus attention on the right-to-death movement. So too did the California law of 1976, which gives the terminally ill the right to die with dignity and without application of "heroic" medical means. But even such measures are subject to more than the will of the patient, as expressed in advance. All forms of death are open to legal scrutiny and control.

Much of the controversy in the area of bioethics might be labeled antiscientific in the sense that it stems from a feeling that science has gone too far. In the cases of abortion and (to a lesser degree) death-with-dignity, however, there is no unanimity of sentiment. Fierce convictions have pitted sections of the general public against each other. One group champions "right of choice" while the other views such a right not as legitimate liberty but as license to murder.

Bioethical considerations were also debated in 1974, when Congress created the National Commission for Protection of Human Subjects of Biomedical and Behavioral Research. That action was largely in response to the outcry that followed news of a long-term study of syphilis, in which a group of blacks (of small means) served as subjects. The commission's vigilance has extended to the roles of the Central Intelligence Agency and the Department of Defense, both of which have been charged with highly questionable practices in what has come to be known as mind control, employing, among other means, hallucinogens and electroshock.

So both the private scientist and the fictional Dr. Strangelove with government connections have been targets of the reform-minded. Whether commissions and even the judiciary are adequate safeguards, however, remains in doubt, as can be seen in the articles reprinted in this compilation. A single advancement of learning seems to spawn a multitude of maddening contingencies, whose handling would tax a Solomon.

Section I, a general survey of the field of bioethics, outlines the moral challenges stemming from advances in biology and medicine. In Section II attention is centered upon the beginning of life: first the ethical and legal considerations that have made abortion—the medical termination of pregnancy—a raging political issue; and second, the questions for science and society posed by medical efforts to bring about conception and pregnancy. The end of life, until very recently a subject shunned as too morbid for general discussion, is necessarily an area of profound moral concern; the decisions, often agonizing, that must be made by physicians, nurses, patients, families, or judicial authorities are dealt with in Section III. The last two sections of the book present arguments relating to the proper management of health resources to preserve life and, finally, the field of genetic experimentation, exciting but risky engineering undertaken to enhance the life of future generations.

The compiler wishes to thank the authors and publishers who have granted permission to reprint the selections in this volume.

BRUCE BOHLE

August 1979

CONTENTS

III. DEATH WITH DIGNITY

IV. THE ETHICAL USE OF MEDICAL RESOURCES

V. GENETIC ENGINEERING: PRESENT HAZARDS,
    FUTURE GAINS

I. BIOETHICAL DILEMMAS: SCIENCE AND HUMAN VALUES

EDITOR'S INTRODUCTION

Although it is a direct outgrowth of precisely documented scientific progress, bioethics itself is strangely resistant to systematic presentation. Only the definition is fairly simple, provided one sticks to general terms and calls it the application of ethics to the life sciences of biology and medicine. But it is more than a matter of keeping up with a proliferation of knowledge, and legislation and court decisions that have followed it. With every advance, it seems, there come (1) manifold problems and (2) a consequent challenge that is at the core of the subject—how to handle the problems in the interest of humanity.

Ethics itself is, in its nature, an amorphous and very subjective topic. Each of us may have a fairly strict idea of what is right in a given set of circumstances, yet getting a consensus is about as simple as manipulating mercury. The proof of that is found in the degree to which abortion has polarized the nation.

The excerpts in this section survey the vast area of bioethics. The first article, by Leonard C. Lewin, is particularly wide-ranging; it introduces all the subjects that are discussed in greater detail in the sections that follow and raises the principal ethical issues posed by those subjects. The challenge is making the right choice between alternatives, usually very difficult ones. Thus advocates of abortion rights are not "*for* abortion," per se, but for choice, for a course that, in their view, is less undesirable. Foes of abortion hold convictions equally strong. Not only are there no easy answers; there are none that could easily be applied to a succession of examples of representative cases within a given subject area, even if a consensus could be arrived at.

In the second article, the editors of *The Futurist* cover the labyrinthine field somewhat more selectively and specifically. Their point of departure is a recent book, Allen R. Utke's *Bio-Babel,* one of hundreds that in a very short time have provided bioethics with a formidable bibliography. (One publication rejected by the scientific community was the well-advertised account of a human cloning, or asexual reproduction of an offspring from the cell of a single parent. Researchers who have experimented with lower plant and animal forms scorned the book as lacking in scientific evidence and dismissed the application of the process to human life as purely speculative.)

The third article in this section, by Dr. Gerald Weissmann, is a scientist's response to current accusations—a plea to allow science, which is not inherently antisocial, to advance "uncensored." In contrast, the theme of the final selection, from *Commonweal,* is that science and technology are dehumanizing if practiced uncritically and without restraint.

POSING THE QUESTIONS [1]

. . . It was probably inevitable that the ethical questions that arise in the life sciences would assume a name that is both convenient and scientistic. (Just plain "ethics" would suffice, and often does, but the philosophical and religious connotations of the simpler term don't sit well with many of the technologists, politicians, and lawyers who must deal with these matters.) By whatever name, bioethical questions have always troubled us—but percep-

[1] From article entitled "Bioethical Questions: Who Lives, Who Dies, and Who Decides?" by Leonard C. Lewin, author of *Report from Iron Mountain* and *Triage. Harper's.* v 257, no 1539, p 21-9. Ag. '78. Reprinted by permission of Wallace & Sheil Agency, Inc., 118 E. 61 St., New York, NY 10021. Copyright © 1978 by Leonard Lewin. First published in *Harper's.*

tions of them change. Today, because the new medicine has made them so much more visible, bioethical questions are being examined more carefully, more extensively, and under a number of broad rubrics. As follows:

Allocation of resources applies not only to all aspects of health care, but also to general social priorities; the problem involves technology, economics, politics, and class interest, as well as ethical values. First of all, to what extent is health defined by medical rather than social criteria? At this point in history, what are reasonable goals in public health? By what criteria should resources be allocated for preventive rather than therapeutic medicine? Or for advancing medical technology rather than extending current technology to more people who need it? Is the *objective* of "health care" to prolong life, improve life's quality (how defined?), increase economic productivity, make life more subjectively enjoyable, or to realize some other goal?

How can public-health resources be distributed fairly? Some American communities have more hospital beds—and more enormously expensive equipment—than they can use. Others are hard put to maintain a resident doctor, much less a hospital. Lavish treatment for some and inadequate care for others is the rule. Can such inequities be remedied without stringent government control of the assignment of doctors, nurses, and equipment?

Should public-health policy seek a minimum decent level for all, or the greatest good for the greatest number, or the best possible average care in a given population? These objectives are by no means the same. Is there a basic *right* to health care, and what services should it encompass? Is it possible to exercise such a right in a medical market economy of fee-for-service and private insurance?

Experimentation. Assuming that a series of experiments promises medical advances that may substantially improve the length or quality of life for many people, under what circumstances is it proper to use other people as test subjects? Must the subjects always be fully informed of the possible side effects and dangers of the experiments? If not, what are ethically proper exceptions? Under what circumstances can prisoners, for example, who may hope to have their sentences commuted by participating in such a program, be considered to have given their free assent? How legitimate are experiments on children, and on others who may not be capable of giving informed consent? Who can speak for them, and in what circumstances?

Recently a new issue has been added to this category: the widely reported controversy on recombinant DNA experiments. The experiments involve changing the genetic structure of microorganisms, and force us to weigh the hazard to the general population that the experiments may pose against the social and scientific benefits that may result. The deeper and perhaps more vexing question attending the controversy is the degree to which scientists should be answerable to, and controlled by, the body politic in the knowledge they pursue and the methods they use. Although a working protocol to govern recombinant DNA experiments appears to have been formulated, the limits of scientific freedom are sure to be debated in other contexts, and perhaps more sharply.

Genetic screening. It is now possible to predict a number of characteristics of unborn children according to the genetic inheritance of their parents or by sampling the amniotic fluid during late pregnancy. The latter procedure —amniocentesis—can reveal certain serious defects such as Down's syndrome (Mongolism) , as well as gender. To what extent is it proper to abort possible or probable defectives or to permit them to come to term? For that matter, should it be permissible for parents thus to "choose" the sex of their next child? Under what circumstances is it justifiable to sterilize people likely—or certain—to produce carriers of disease or of other unwanted traits? How does one reconcile the desire or "right" of people to bear defective children with the opposing societal interest? And at what point are defective characteristics deemed sufficiently "undesirable" that society's interest must prevail?

Death and dying. It is by now generally accepted that any person has the right to refuse treatment, for himself at least, and for whatever reason, even when such a decision is tantamount to suicide. (Yet suicide itself is illegal in most jurisdictions, and an attempt at suicide is often considered prima facie evidence of mental incompetence.) But do people also have a right to *receive* maximum, or extraordinary, treatment in order to survive? As for rejecting treatment, it is one thing to make such a decision when fully competent to do so, but this is not usually the case for a patient already in extremis, who may be in a coma, heavily drugged, deeply depressed—or for an infant. How is competence then determined, and by whom? Who makes the decision for the patient when he cannot make his wishes known? A predesignated surrogate? Lacking that, his next of kin? Lacking that or anyone else close enough to claim or accept responsibility, should the decision be entrusted to a hospital ethics committee, an attending physician, or a court?

During World War II, penicillin was new and scarce. Given the choice of treating the possibly mortal infections of the critically injured and treating venereal disease in soldiers who could be returned to combat, the latter was given preference. When resources are at hand to save one patient and two patients need them, whose life is judged more valuable, and by what criteria? The very young, the mature, those in the prime of life, those with the best prospects for a satisfactory life, those judged to have more to contribute to society? And, of course, who makes the judgment?

Euthanasia, which used to mean simply a "happy death," has come to mean abetting the death of someone who wants to die, usually someone for whom life does not seem worth the pain or emptiness it will hold. "Active" euthanasia, such as giving a patient a lethal injection, is murder according to the law; "passive" euthanasia, such as discontinuing treatment, is not usually so considered. But is it morally legitimate to distinguish the two?

Population control. Genetic screening, in the sense used earlier, is population control on a very limited scale. Voluntary contraception and sterilization, as well as elective abortion, also serve to lower the birth rate; the ethical questions they imply turn on individual rights. But what of large-scale compulsory control of reproduction, where an important societal interest is asserted? The prevailing view—by no means unchallenged, to be sure—sees the rate of population increase running well ahead of the production of resources necessary to sustain it. Doomsday projections have encouraged open discussion of the so-called lifeboat ethic, in which the world is analogous to an overloaded lifeboat from which a number of passengers must be cast for the rest to survive. The term "triage," once used only in military medicine to describe the selection on the battlefield of whom to treat and whom to abandon, now extends beyond even general hospital practice to embrace a wider social predicament: Where and on what basis will an effort be made to save endangered peoples, and where not?

The highest birth rates, by and large, occur in the parts of the world least able to support them. Yet in such areas programs to promote voluntary methods of birth control have not been popular. Mrs. Gandhi's aggressive promotion of sterilization in India contributed significantly to her political defeat . . . [in 1977]. The response of the wealthy nations to mass famine in Bangladesh and in the African Sahel a few years ago was limited at best; perhaps the fact that any response is made at all represents an ethical advance in international responsibility. But one suspects that the pessimism with which wealthy nations view the survival of their impoverished neighbors masks an unarticulated willingness to let these people go over the sides of the life-boat.

This most profound bioethical question will be with us for a long time: To what extent does a national or inter-national "right" to control available resources supersede individual "rights" to bear children?

Transplants. After Dr. Christiaan Barnard performed the first heart transplant operation in 1967, a macabre satirical vision of eager, knife-bearing surgeons stalking the terminal wards and the emergency rooms gained cur-rency. And, in fact, a black market in kidneys has been reported, and it's a fair guess that the same thing will happen for other essential organs as it becomes possible to transplant them. Selling organs, tissue, and blood to the highest bidder is clearly venal. More ethically ambiguous (according to the increasingly accepted new criterion of "brain death") is the deliberate maintenance, as a source of spare parts, of the pulsing, breathing bodies of people deemed "legally" dead. Indeed, a Boston physician has premised a thriller, entitled *Coma,* on just this strategy. . . .

Role of the Bioethicist

Bioethicists—usually physicians, philosophers, theolo-gians, lawyers, nurses, and public-health activists—are deeply engaged in examining these kinds of issues. Many of them deplore the label for its suggestion that bioethics is an established profession, or for its implication that any-one can claim expert knowledge of what is right and what is wrong. But bioethics is a discipline—however "soft"—and, as the kinds of questions cited here should indicate, it is being applied ever more widely.

The acknowledged center of activity is the Institute of Society, Ethics and the Life Sciences, more commonly known as the Hastings Center, in Hastings-on-Hudson, New York. Organized less than ten years ago by Daniel Callahan, a philosopher, and Willard Gaylin, . . . [a] psy-chiatrist . . . , the center has extended its activities and influence to a growing number of the nation's medical and law schools, and it maintains several continuing programs of research and education. Its bimonthly *Hastings Center Report* is the principal publication in the field.

So the bioethicists think, talk, write, study, and teach—and to what end, if *not* to determine the answers to these questions? I would say that the bioethicists' first concern is consciousness-raising (to use the locution chiefly associated with the women's movement): developing a greater awareness of the ethical issues in, for example, medical practice. At Hastings they call it "complexifying" the issues—trying to take every interest and point of view into account—in order, paradoxically, to clarify them.

The bioethicists are increasingly in demand as consultants: organizing seminars and teaching programs in professional and other schools, helping groups who must decide health policy, drafting legislation, and, on occasion, helping to set up hospital ethics or review committees. These latter groups (as distinguished from purely professional prognosis committees) have been looked to by some laypersons as possible arbitrators of the decisions to begin or discontinue extreme efforts to maintain life. Robert M. Veatch, the Hastings senior associate in charge of its continuing program on death and dying, believes that such authority would be ethically undesirable, even if made legally unambiguous, because it begs the question of where responsibility should lie. Ethics committees, he feels, should be able to provide useful perspective—as a resource for physicians, patients, relatives, and others concerned—but not final judgments.

Even the most simply phrased bioethical question usually requires an inordinate amount of "complexifying" before persuasive alternatives begin to emerge. But a number of broad common denominators are manifest in *all* the questions posed here. *Rights,* for one example: of the individual, the family, the professional, the institution, the state, the society. It would be convenient indeed if rights did not so often conflict. (And to what extent is a "right" an ethical imperative rather than a legal or political concept?) *Responsibilities,* for another: of professional to client, of institution to individual, of citizen to society, of A to B—and the reverse of each. Who should make which decisions, on what authority, to whom accountable? *The value of life:* Who can determine it, and by what criteria? How can one life be measured against another? Can there be—or must there be, for purposes of social policy—a dollar value attached to it? *Politics and economics:* How can existing inequities be substantially mitigated within the current social structure? To what extent are they morally acceptable? Is it possible to have a reasonably "good" society in an economy in which one person usually stands to gain only at the expense of another? Will the continuing biological revolution tend to promote a new, more equitable social contract, or to rationalize the advantages of the already privileged?

Large questions, indeed, for those who have to decide —right now—whether one patient or another is assigned the last bed in the intensive care unit, or if and when to pull the plug, or how to control experiments on some promising new drug. But they—and we—have to start thinking about them. The questions won't get any easier.

SURVIVING THE NEW BIOLOGY [2]

Advances in the biological sciences have a momentum of their own. Separately, the individual discoveries, as remarkable as they may be, are probably controllable and most often beneficial. But collectively they form a complex and perhaps unsturdy tower of change. Discoveries build on each other—sometimes with amazing speed.

Many of the questions that these advances raise are not strictly scientific. In fact, coping with the various scientific

[2] Article from *The Futurist.* v 12, no 5, p 331-2. O. '78. Published by the World Future Society, 4916 St. Elmo Ave., Washington, D.C. 20014.

implications of any new breakthrough may be a comparatively easy task. The social, moral and ethical ramifications of scientific breakthroughs are often more troubling. Chemist Allen R. Utke, author of the new book *Bio-Babel; Can We Survive the New Biology?* [Atlanta, John Knox Press, 1978] believes there is much to be troubled about.

Utke outlines dozens of scientific advances, including:

—*Artificial inovulation.* "Incubator cows" carrying fertilized eggs from other cows have given birth to healthy calves. The first authenticated case of the birth of an artificially inovulated human baby occurred in England on July 25, 1978, when Mrs. Lesley Brown gave birth to her daughter Louise by caesarean section.

—*Parthenogenesis (cloning).* Healthy, living carrots, tobacco plants, asparagus, and frogs have been created by removing a cell or cells from a parent organism and chemically inducing them to multiply until an exact duplicate of the parent was reproduced.

—*Regeneration.* Spinal tissue was regenerated in a paralyzed boy, allowing him to regain the use of his legs.

—*Chemical memory.* Flatworms were taught to respond to flashes of light and then cut in half. Both halves regenerated themselves and "remembered their lessons." Other trained flatworms were ground up and fed to untrained worms and "the cannibalistic worms acquired some of the trained worms' knowledge."

These advances have already been made. More surprising still are many "works in progress," the most notorious of which is probably the current research on recombinant DNA. In these experiments, the basic chromosomal structure of bacteria is changed, producing new strains. Scientists and laymen alike fear that one of these new bacteria might prove resistant to known antibacterial medicines and cause an epidemic if it escaped from the laboratory.

Studies like these bring scientists close to the mystery of life itself. In fact, Utke cites British physicist J. D. Bernal as one who sees life hardly as a mystery at all. In Bernal's words, life is becoming "a cryptogram, a puzzle, a code that can be broken, a working model that can sooner or later be built." Discoveries of amino acids, the basic components of proteins, on remnants of meteorites have led some scientists to theorize that life is actually inevitable—one of the properties of matter. Cyril Ponnamperuma, an origins of life researcher also quoted in this book, says,

People used to think that the primeval elements had to sit around in the ocean for millions of years before something happened. We now know that once the right molecules accumulated at the right time and in the right arrangement, life could begin almost instantaneously. Evolution is what takes time.

Utke also outlines the kinds of new advances people can expect in the next few years. By 1985 he anticipates artificial insemination with the choice of the child's sex and a limited number of personality traits, the conquering of cancer, the production of artificial viruses, the use of hibernation drugs, and pain relief through electronic stimulation of the brain. By the year 2000, Utke expects there will be artificial wombs, frozen organ banks, tissue regeneration, the synthesis of single-celled animals, the discovery of extraterrestrial life, disembodied animal and human brains (cyborgs), and computerized knowledge and memory boosters implanted in the brain.

But in Utke's view, many of these developments cause more problems than they solve. He has many questions for the scientists and even the societies involved. For example, do people have the inalienable right to have children—even if overpopulation becomes critical? Do the deformed, the retarded, and the genetically ill have the right to reproduce? Do parents have the right to choose the sex of their offspring? Should society collect sperm samples from its most intelligent or talented members and use them for artificial insemination? If an aborted fetus is alive after an abortion, should doctors attempt to keep it alive? If not, should they be allowed to experiment on it while it remains alive? These are questions that demand prompt answers, according to Utke. They are dilemmas of the present. But they are only the tip of the iceberg. Before satisfactory answers to these questions can be found, advances in the life sciences are certain to pose new questions that are equally urgent.

Many people have called for a national or international "science court" to study new scientific developments, but Utke argues that such an organization would probably not be empowered to make policy decisions, and at best would become a clearinghouse for scientific information.

Utke's proposed alternative is a 10-year moratorium on "artificial inovulation research, the development of artificial wombs, attempts to clone small mammals and humans, cell fusion experiments, and recombinant DNA research." In his view, the dangers involved in experimenting in these areas far outweigh any foreseeable benefits. He argues in favor of group pressure to stop further research of this kind. "Educational groups, organized religion, environmental groups, and the League of Women Voters" are the kinds of organizations Utke hopes will support such a moratorium.

Obstacles to concerted action remain, though. The general public, according to Utke, feels that the government, or even science itself, will always bail them out. People are too optimistic and too proud, in Utke's view. Utke believes that man is indeed a superior animal, but one who has become too sure of his superiority. Man does not lack ingenuity, Utke says, but wisdom. Science is building a biological Tower of Babel, and Utke fears that history will repeat itself.

SCIENCE FOR SCIENCE'S SAKE [3]

"Resolved that there are some things biological scientists ought not to know, because if they know them, our sense of

[3] Article entitled "Give Me Liberty," by Gerald Weissmann, professor of medicine and director, Division of Rheumatology, New York University Medical Center, and author and editor of books on research medicine and cell biology. *The Sciences.* v 19, p 22-4. Ja. '79. © 1979 by The New York Academy of Sciences.

what is human will be violated." That, in its simplest form, is the subject of the current debate now going on not only among biologists but in the U.S. Senate, symposia on ethics, and in the editorial columns of *Nature*.

Until recently biomedical scientists have been quite certain that any new knowledge they acquired about the nature of living things could not help but be useful to the general welfare, and that such "utilitarian" values constituted a moral guarantee for their intrusions upon the natural world. In consequence, they only had to follow their "esthetic" concerns in pursuit of the elegant experiment, the beautiful proof, the unshakable theory. Recent events have unsettled this agreeable view.

There is ample support for the idea that "science-for-its-own-sake," the esthetic view of science, yields utilitarian benefits. Research looking not so much for a cure for disease, but rather seeking the nature of soil fungi, gave us streptomycin. Inquiry into the nature of cells in culture led to the Salk vaccine. And studies of the cell cycle in onion root tips have suggested a rational treatment of leukemia. Such examples, and at least three-score others which decorate our recent history, have reassured biological scientists that the enterprise is intrinsically benign. As a corollary, scientists have persuaded themselves that if they perform their task professionally—by doing well—they do good.

Their doubts relieved as to ends, the biomedical scientist concentrates on means. And what magnificent means they are! The toyshops of technology, and the purses of our government, have provided biologists with electron microscopes to view single cells peeled and split like oranges, centrifuges which hurl viruses at gravitational forces a hundred-thousand-fold that of the Earth, x-rays which display the molecular symmetry of our tendons and spectrophotometers which scan the uncoiling of our genes.

By these means, the game of science has been played in obedience to a set of rules which has remained uncluttered by any ethical stricture save one: *thou shalt not fudge the data.* The professional code of the scientist has been a stringently esthetic one. It has rewarded the individual imagination for coming up with reproducible experiments. And that kind of imagination has, until recently, been considered by one and all to resemble that of the creative artist, no more—and no less—in the service of temporal, social mores.

W. H. Auden summed it up this way: "Both science and art are primarily spiritual activities, whatever practical applications may be derived from their results."

The Challenge

But all this has now become so strongly challenged that the esthetic values of biomedical research have been edged into disrepute. Indeed, even the utilitarian ends of science—the manipulation of nature for the eradication of what we perceive as its errors—have been attacked by environmentalists, humanists and the new theologians. Energized a decade ago by the folly of our technology in Vietnam (organic herbicides against the tropical forest, psychoactive drugs in the hands of the CIA), critics from without have been joined by the disenchanted young from within the perimeter of science, culminating in the latest fuss over recombinant DNA. What began as a brave, internal effort to face the ethical problems raised by gene-splicing has slowly developed into a broad social movement to proscribe certain kinds of inquiry. For the first time in recent Western history, there is a good chance that some, perhaps benign, authority will legally declare to the biological scientist: thou shalt not do this experiment, because it is *morally* wrong to muck about with our genes.

Rather than rehearse the scenarios of gloom that opponents of DNA recombinancy have plotted, let us use the categories of Harvard biologist Bernard Davis, who claims that they retell three popular myths: the Andromeda-strain fantasy, the legend of chimeras, and the creation of the Golem. Nor will I go into the overwhelming evidence that these myths are unlikely to be realized. Indeed, they become more improbable with each new issue of *Science* or

Nature, as the solid experimental advances of January render pointless the regulatory legislation drafted in October [1978].

Instead, let us turn to a friendly critic, June Goodfield, whose recent book, *Playing God* (Random House, 1977), recounts the history of the genetic debate, and elaborates upon its larger meaning. Admitting that ". . . it is so hard to produce a *rational* argument for one's moral qualms about DNA research," she nevertheless encapsulates the less-than-rational ones which are so much more powerful:

> What bothered us so about the new technology? Three things came to mind: the slow erosion of that which up to this point in our history has gone to make us uniquely human, or what we have considered to be human; the latterday assault on personal autonomy and integrity; and the increasing sense that individuals are losing control over the conduct and direction of human affairs.

I hope it is not fanciful to point out that the first of these worries is a restatement of the Golem fantasy, the second a rephrasing of the chimera myth (assault on personal integrity), and the third reflects a modest confusion between *Brave New World* and *The Double Helix.* But this reduction of Goodfield's arguments does not render them less cogent. Scientists share with humanists these worries as to the remote, unpleasant, utilitarian consequences of gene-splicing, even as they exult over their recent capacity to turn bacteria into engines for production of insulin or somatostatin.

But the most striking extension of these social and ethical anxieties is yet to come, for as the philosopher A. J. Ayer has suggested: ". . . ethical terms do not serve only to *express* feelings. They are calculated also to *arouse* feeling, and so to stimulate action" [my emphasis].

Utilitarian and Esthetic Values

The action which is called for conflicts with both the utilitarian and esthetic values of biomedical research. It is the imposition, by means of external authority, of a *pro-*

fessional code upon the scientist. Such a code, arrived at by the "usual" democratic process, and with the "usual" degree of consent by the regulated, will guarantee—we may presume—that after their successful pursuit of the Golden Fleece researchers will not come home to Medea. These professional codes (as fairly arrived at as the codicils of Internal Revenue) will not only enlarge the number of degree-bearers now legislatively responsible for the products of their endeavors, but also submit these to moral scrutiny.

In the cautions of legislators and ethical philosophers we can discern that the moral imperative for regulation comes from abuse (even if only potential) and the abuse biologists stand accused of is their capacity to fiddle with genes. Such arguments go on to urge not only that professional scientists should be governed by some sort of professional guild—like the American Medical Association or the American Bar Association—but that they should be subject to the laws of malpractice.

Goodfield describes the unregulated state of science before our recent, ethical concerns:

Save for the expenditure of society's funds, however, the [scientific] profession was still accountable for nothing. The law in no way held them to the highest degree of care: they were never sued for malpractice nor for misapplication of their work. The only set of ethical principles that ever concerned them were those concerned with protecting the good name of the profession and its "sublime" methodology. They were in no way concerned with the needs of society . . . .

This argument assumes that scientists' utilitarian output has some unique social implications, and that these implications require society at large to set some limit on their esthetically motivated quest. But are the social consequences of scientific research different in kind from those of other scholarly pursuits or from the creative arts?

Professional historians, for example, suggest that the utility of their narratives provides us with an understanding of the present; professional philosophers often believe that the usefulness of their metier leads us to proper conduct; and social scientists agree that their analyses are of use in the amelioration of political problems. But can we say with certainty that the contributions of Fichte, Nietzsche and Spengler had less grave consequences for the orderly flow of social progress than even the most lurid results imaginable of our biologic inquiries? Should the esthetic motivations of Pound, Céline or the Marquis de Sade have been modulated at the source by a morals committee? Cyril Connolly has quipped: *"Le coeur à ses raisons* —and so have rheumatism and the 'flu'."

Since some of us look into the reasons of rheumatism for the reasons of our heart, is it extravagant for the sciences to claim—at least with respect to subject matter—a measure of the license granted to the arts?

Censorship and Liberty

Like it or not, we are discussing censorship when we liken the profession of science to the profession of law or of medicine. Malpractice rules are written to ensure that the practitioner conforms to the general level of professional practice in the community—surely this is *not* the standard of creative scientists, nor of innovative scholars in any field. The possible misuses, in the utilitarian sense, of their knowledge should, in my view, not lead to preemptive rules as to the kind of inquiry in which the professional engages. Scientists, in the best interpretation, are not *only* professionals in the sense that lawyers or doctors are. In the best sense, they are professionals in the way of historians, poets or artists.

Let me advance this claim, as phrased by Auden:

Liberty is prior to virtue; i.e. liberty cannot be distinguished from license, for freedom of choice is neither good nor bad, but the human prerequisite without which virtue and vice have no meaning. Virtue is, of course, preferable to vice but to choose vice is preferable to having virtue chosen for one.

Such a completely libertarian view is clearly counter to the temper of our time. We must, indeed, accept the rational bases for the general disenchantment of our culture with the products of science pursued for its own ends. The wonderful folks who gave you (however indirectly) the bomb of Hiroshima, the laboratory of Auschwitz and the psychiatry of the Gulag archipelago are not generally trusted to keep their new genetic tools locked safely in the academic cupboard.

But from where did the counterforces arise to these overt excesses? To a large extent, scientists themselves, acting in response to a code of moral values they share with others, have "blown the whistle" on more of these outrages. The atomic scientists, by means of their *Bulletin,* have resisted the proliferation of their monster, biomedical scientists have propagated the Nuremberg Declaration and the psychiatrists have exposed the social mischief of the mental health commissars. The motivating force behind these ameliorative actions has been, I believe, the sense of humane ethics with which our society at large is impregnated.

Our only guarantee that new knowledge will not be gained at the expense of human values is the integrity of that network of values in which all our inquiries are enmeshed. This is to argue that we should impose no pre-emptive restrictions on the kinds of new knowledge to be sought. If we wish, for example, to prohibit certain investigations on human subjects by our physiologists because their Nazi counterparts violated any reasonable code of behavior, we may be granting the Nazis a posthumous victory they do not deserve. Of course, science should not design experiments that are trivial, dangerous or dehumanizing. However, these adjectives are best defined by the consensus of society at large. If that consensus be justly derived, we can expect that the community of scientists, as citizens, will agree.

The British scholar George Steiner has recently argued that "truth at any price"—unrestricted inquiry into anything at all at any time—is an over-riding cultural value of our sort of civilization. It may well be, but only to the extent that it does not entirely conflict with those values of society that scientists themselves have introjected. There are many "truths" and many kinds of knowledge—and if we want to be sure that scientists (following their own esthetic bents) do not come up with chimeras or Golems, we'd be well-advised to make certain that our society as a whole doesn't want such fantasies realized. The alternative—the proscription of those lines of inquiry which could possibly lead to chimeras or Golems—is based on the assumptions that only the *worst* consequences of an experiment are to be expected. Many of us over forty would not be alive today if that assumption had been dominant in the last century.

Finally, many of us are convinced that the culture of science, which engages at least as much of our population as does the humanist culture, is worth nurturing for its own sake. The unraveling of the genetic code, the elucidation of cell structure and metabolism, the analysis of how nerves make muscles twitch or speech possible, constitute cultural achievements no less imposing than the mosaics of Ravenna or the cathedrals of France. At a time when the arts of our decade are devoted to the production and analysis of works related to self, the objective triumphs of our science are perhaps even more to be cherished. We are, probably, unlikely to achieve the utilitarian ends of our science: freedom from hunger and disease, less anxious youth and sturdy age, without adopting the risky, libertarian view that there shall be no bounds as to what scientists need to know. Motivated by esthetic considerations to reach the aims of utility, new biomedical knowledge will come—in the words of Sloan-Kettering's Lewis Thomas, ". . . if the air is right . . . in its own season, like pure honey."

A TRIUMPH OF TECHNOLOGY [4]

Much more than the fictional dictatorship of the computer "Hal" in the movie 2001, the trial of Karen Quinlan

[4] Article by Thomas A. Shannon, assistant professor of social ethics, Dept. of Humanities, Worcester Polytechnic Institute. *Commonweal.* v 102, no 19, p 589-90. D. 5, '75.

may well have revealed something of the real relation between humans and technology. Indeed, the decision that Ms. Quinlan must be artificially maintained by her respirator may be a clear signal that humans stand in a new relation to technology and the products of a technological civilization.

Humanity has spent the last few centuries rejoicing in its freedom from the domination by the powers of nature. Now it may suddenly find its position reversed. Only this time the dependency may be a creature of humanity's own making. One reason for this is because of what many have called the "technological imperative." Simply stated, this means that if we can do it, we should do it. In many ways, this imperative lies close to the heart of America for it stresses the virtues of pragmatism, activism and capitalism. But if it is allowed to operate uncritically, we may find that it will bring us closer to the science-fiction fantasies of the totally technological society.

Of all the many questions that have been raised by the Quinlan case, the question of the technological imperative may be the most important, for it sets forth the basic ethical and social context in which all other questions have to be asked. However, it is the imperative itself that needs critical evaluation. In many ways, it has been a working hypothesis of contemporary society and of health care in particular. While technology may be forcing ethics to re-evaluate some of its principles and conclusions, ethics must also force such a re-evaluation of the basic premises of technology so that the values can be clearly stated and their operational consequences can be evaluated.

The principle of the technological imperative is extremely critical in the Quinlan matter for it shapes almost preconsciously our feelings and value-responses about the situation. If it is evident that we can continue to maintain Ms. Quinlan on a respirator almost indefinitely—and there is the technological capacity to do so—then who are her parents, or anyone else for that matter, to demand that the machine be turned off? What right do we have to terminate what technology can prolong?

What has happened in this process is a subtle—but extremely critical—reversal of the traditional question about the use of extraordinary or heroic means of treatment. Traditionally, the ethical task has been to justify the use of extraordinary means of therapy or treatment. In the usual ethical interpretation, extraordinary has meant very expensive, experimental, or medicine proper to the disease, but which is incapable of restoring the person to health. The principle has always recognized that what is extraordinary can become ordinary; but it still clings to the test of the potential for restoring health for evaluating the treatment. Pius XII—no flaming liberal—argued that one was never obligated to use such means even though death would certainly and knowingly follow. The basic reason is that the ethical tradition saw people as bound to use only what would be ordinarily required to maintain health. And, at least in the Catholic tradition, there is the recognition that life is not the highest value and that, therefore, one is not obligated to do what is extraordinary to preserve it. From this framework, one can fairly easily argue that Ms. Quinlan need not be maintained on the respirator. It is an extremely expensive procedure and on that basis alone very extraordinary. Also the treatment—including the use of the respirator—has no potential to restore her to health. It is very important to recognize that there have been no medical claims that she will ever be cured or restored to a meaningful degree of health, even though her physical life may be maintained.

However, an extremely important shift seems to have taken place. A working presupposition of many connected with the trial seems to have been the preservation of life for its own sake. The major reason for this may be that we now have the technological capacity to prolong life almost indefinitely. The question has been moved from whether we should turn the machine on to whether we should turn it off. The problem of whether this treatment may be extraordinary or beneficial seems to have vanished. Very little emphasis is being placed on whether Ms. Quinlan's treatment may have any benefits to her—other than artificially maintaining her at a rather low level of even physical existence, to say nothing of the quality of her personal life. Part of the reason for this shift in orientation may be the simple presence of the machines in the hospitals. We have them and therefore we use them. Another reason may be that such technological advances represent a way of avoiding our embarrassment over death, for we now have a way to put off this final affront to modern medicine. A final reason may be the uncritical and unexamined acceptance of such technological advances as an unqualified good. We have designed the machines; they work exceptionally well; therefore they and their effects must be good. When stated in such a form, the technological imperative is easily recognized as illogical. But when disguised as modern medical care and treatment, it may not appear in this unfavorable light. But however one interprets this major shift in the ethical analysis of such cases, there must be an evaluation, for a shift such as this is too important an issue to enter our lives uncritically.

A triumph of technology will occur if the technological imperative is not brought forward and clearly examined. But this most basic question was not called into question at the trial. The problem of active vs. passive euthanasia, the degree of control humans have over their own lives and the lives of others, the specter of a renewal of Nazi-type atrocities, and the Vatican's last desperate grasp at control over the destiny of individuals all pale in comparison to the problem of determining whether we ought to do all that we can. To make such a decision uncritically or on the basis of some false issues raised in the Quinlan case would be the greatest of follies and the most unethical of all possibilities.

The Quinlan case represents an important crossroad for humanity. For the decision that the machine should not be turned off may mean that we are entering a new age and will find ourselves in a new relation to technology. If the right to terminate such treatment had been upheld, humanity would have been affirmed as the master of the technology it designs, rather than its servant. As it is, the fate of Ms. Quinlan may reveal much about ourselves and our future.

[The court decision was reversed, but Karen Quinlan has managed to survive without the aid of the respirator—Ed.]

II. THE BEGINNING OF LIFE

EDITOR'S INTRODUCTION

Abortion: Biology and Politics

The arguments raised by the legalization of abortion grapple with the most basic questions concerning the beginning of life. When does human life "begin"? Is it ever right and necessary to terminate a pregnancy? Who is to make the decision? What governmental controls are required? Supporters and opponents of abortion rights, equally vehement, have made the question of these rights as much a political issue as a personal and medical decision for patient and physician. Ethics and religious or moral convictions are at the bottom of the politics, along with contentious emotion. An absolute "right to life" or a woman's "right to choose": these are the grounds on which the adversaries stand. The selections in the first part of this divided section, which deal with abortion, make it clear that in this controversy the focus is only partly scientific. Solutions are sought in judicial, legislative, and—ultimately—political action.

Before the 1970s, illegal operations or abortions in foreign countries for those who could afford them were the only options available. As the decade began, rigid state controls had made legal abortion off limits to any American woman not in grave physical danger as a result of a pregnancy. There were, however, some stirrings to indicate a desire for liberalized laws. Many—not all of them activists of the women's movement—demanded the right of all women, rich or poor, to choose safe, legal termination of pregnancy. The danger of extreme birth defects resulting from hazardous medication or disease during pregnancy intensified the demand.

On January 22, 1973, the Supreme Court struck down virtually all existing state legislation on abortion. The decision reflected the approach to abortion that distinguishes states of pregnancy—and thus reflects the judgment that in the final stage the fetus is capable of life outside the womb. In the first three months (trimester), the court ruled, there could be no state interference with abortion, except for a requirement that it be performed by a physician. In the second three-month period, states were given certain controls over medical aspects, in the interest of the woman's safety; but, again, they were forbidden to limit the reasons for which the abortion was performed—such limitation being a violation of the right of privacy guaranteed by the Constitution. Only in the final three-month period could a state ban an abortion other than one performed to save the mother's life.

And so a national abortion policy was born. The 1973 court decision has remained the basic law of the land, yet implementation of the decision has often proved difficult. Though the effect of the ruling was to make abortions the most frequently performed surgery in the United States, from the outset only certain parts of the country, notably the Northeast and California, together with large cities in general, were areas in which abortion was readily available.

On July 1, 1976, other Supreme Court decisions widened abortion rights by ruling out requirements for consent by husbands or by parents of minors. A measure of state control was retained, however, and as a result, there has followed a stream of legislation aimed especially at preventing teen-age abortions. Another landmark decision was the June 20, 1977, Supreme Court ruling that states and localities were not required by the Constitution to pay for elective abortions (those not dictated by strong *medical* reasons affecting the welfare of mother and unborn child). The 1977 ruling was as decisive as the 1973 one had been. Many viewed the new ruling as not incompatible with the earlier one; others contended that the rights won in 1973 were nullified for indigent residents of states denying assistance: without funds for private medical care or for travel, they might, as in earlier times, resort to quacks.

Although the volume of legal abortion has increased steadily since 1973, the effect of the 1977 decision on federal funding (through the Medicaid program) has been very great. And since 1977 federal standards for funding abortion have been increasingly stringent; only cases involving rape, incest, or a threat to a woman's life or health have been certified. Most of the states have been no more liberal (though there have been exceptions to account for the continuing national rise in abortion).

Abortion remains an ongoing political issue, with the prevailing pattern fairly clear. Despite a well-organized effort, the "pro-life" group (supporters of fetal rights and opponents of abortion in general) has not succeeded in overturning the 1973 ruling. The "pro-choice" faction (supporters of women's rights to reproductive freedom and to safe, elective abortions regardless of financial means) is equally short of its goal. And so about a dozen national organizations employing, as a rule, either "right to life" or "abortion rights" in their names, continue the struggle.

Many of the foes of abortion seek to reverse the 1973 ruling by means of a constitutional amendment banning abortion. By the middle of 1979, fifteen states had made petitions for a convention that would consider the ban, thirty-four (two thirds) being the number needed to clear the first hurdle, beyond which looms the requirement of ratification of the amendment by three fourths of the states. Few observers discount the political efforts of the right-to-life forces. By early 1976, antiabortionist Ellen McCormack of New York State was regularly entering Democratic presidential primaries as a single-issue candidate. In fourteen contests, she claimed 245,000 votes. For the November election, the Republicans adopted a platform favoring the constitutional amendment; the Democrats opposed the amendment. Both Gerald Ford and Jimmy Carter found the issue a difficult one.

In the congressional elections of 1978, pro-life activists contended that they had played a major role in the defeat of two incumbent senators, Dick Clark of Iowa and Thomas

McIntyre of New Hampshire. In New York State, a new party, Right to Life, made its first election bid an impressive one. Its candidate for governor, Mary Jane Tobin, outpolled the well-established Liberal Party, which had endorsed the successful Democratic incumbent, Hugh Carey. And in June 1979 the first announced candidate for the 1980 Democratic presidential nomination was an antiabortion activist, Sean Morton Downey, who declared that the incumbent leadership had turned his party into "the party of death." In the face of such determined efforts, the pro-choice forces renewed their own efforts, though much less visibly.

Not all the antiabortion activity since 1973 has been confined to the hustings: abortion clinics themselves have been the scenes of raids and demonstrations. And opposition has frequently been violent; when a clinic in Hempstead, New York, was torched in February 1979 the New York *Times* reported that it was the twenty-fifth such occurrence, nationwide.

The first of the five selections on abortion in this section is a *Time* survey of the struggle in July 1979. The second, an essay, also from *Time,* reflects the post-1977 picture while examining the moral/ethical issues of both sides. Two newspaper editorials, from the Birmingham *News* and the St. Louis *Post-Dispatch,* comment on the historic 1973 Supreme Court decision from opposite points of view. The final article on abortion, from the magazine *Human Behavior,* is based on a poll of national attitudes and detects some subtle changes in what is one of the most emotionally charged issues of the day.

Artificial Insemination and In Vitro *Fertilization*

The focus of the second part of this section is on medical efforts to aid reproduction. Compared with that surrounding abortion, the emotional climate of discussions of artificial insemination and *in vitro* fertilization (the "test-tube" baby procedure) seems almost placid.

The human application of artificial insemination goes

back two centuries, and it is still controversial. One quite
recent development in AI is increasing use of sperm banks;
from the American Association for the Advancement of
Science came word in 1979 that the frozen sperm from such
banks is currently used in from 10 to 20 percent of the
cases reported.

So-called test-tube births, in contrast, are quite new. The
pioneer case announced in England in the summer of 1978
was a major news event. Predictably, with it came an array
of bioethical concerns; but, in part because it was an ocean
distant, the event seemed to have less immediate impact in
the United States.

All the same, the opening of the first American clinic
for *in vitro* experimentation, in Norfolk, Virginia, not long
afterward stirred some controversy. Such experiments in
federally funded American institutions are subject to the
approval of the Ethics Advisory Board of the Department
of Health, Education and Welfare. By early 1979, guidelines
had not been firmly established. In private practice, moreover, the specter of malpractice suits tended to act as a
deterrent.

The first of the selections on new techniques, by Peter
Gwynne, concentrates on the celebrated British case. The
second, by Albert Rosenfeld, examines both *in vitro* fertilization and artificial insemination, with emphasis on the
"test-tube" technique. The third, an editorial from *Commonweal*, examines three possible bioethical reactions to
the *in vitro* technique and recommends a middle course.
Next a *Time* article examines various religious responses
to the technique. The final extract, by biochemist David G.
Lygre, examines the biological and ethical aspects of
artificial insemination.

THE ABORTION FIGHT [1]

"Our hero, Henry Hyde!" shouted the speaker last week at a rally in Cincinnati's Fountain Square. As the portly Republican Congressman from Illinois stepped to the rostrum, the crowd of 3,500 chanted: "Life! Life! Life!" · Elderly women wearing white gloves held up red roses. Men lifted up small children. "We're here to remind America of its soul," declared the silver-haired Hyde. "Religious ideals have always guided our country." When he was done speaking, members of the audience began another cadenced cheer: "We're for life, and we couldn't be prouder. Get a little closer, and we'll yell a little louder!" Finally a defiant roar: "No compromise! No compromise!"

The issue was abortion, and the fight was supposed to have been settled in 1973 when the US Supreme Court ruled that a state may not prevent a woman from having an abortion during the first six months of pregnancy until the fetus is presumably capable of "meaningful life outside the mother's womb." But as the passionate cries in Fountain Square showed, the battle is far from over. The rally capped a convention in which the forces opposed to abortion spent most of four days planning strategy for next year's elections and state legislative sessions. In heaping praise on Hyde, they honored a politician who was responsible for one of their most important victories: a 1976 amendment that effectively cut off nearly all federal financing of abortions.

Not far away, on the edge of the Ohio River, some 2,000 men and women staged counterdemonstrations. They carried white carnations and sang: "Fighting for our women, we shall not be moved. Just like a tree that's planted by the water, we shall not be moved." They placed coat hangers at the motel doors of the pro-life supporters, with

[1] From article entitled "The Fanatical Abortion Fight." *Time.* v 114, no 2, p 26-7. Jl. 9, '79. Reprinted by permission from TIME, The Weekly Newsmagazine; Copyright Time Inc. 1979.

signs reading NO MORE COAT HANGER ABORTIONS. They even
tacked a "proclamation of religious liberty" onto the pillar
of St. Peter in Chains Cathedral to protest what they consider the Roman Catholic Church's attempts to coerce all
Americans into following the church's teachings against
abortion.

Across the country, the battle is turning increasingly
political and is waged by men and women who offer no
quarter. It is a fierce clash of fundamental beliefs in which
name calling is considered as potent as reasoned argument.
Thus the antiabortionists call themselves "pro-lifers" and
denounce their opponents as "baby killers." Those who
support a woman's right to abortion call themselves "pro-
choice" and deride the other side as "compulsory pregnancy
people."

Although both sides are equally matched in rhetoric,
the advantage on the field had been held for several years
by the pro-choice forces, fighting mainly in the courts. Now
the momentum has swung to the pro-life groups, and the
struggle has shifted to the political arena. The pro-lifers
operate on the premise that in a close election, a single-
issue group's ability to arouse legions of morally and religiously inspired campaign workers and voters can provide
a decisive edge at the polls. The beneficiaries are usually
conservative candidates. Moreover, to increase their clout,
the pro-lifers are forging a coalition with other conservative
groups, including opponents of gun control, the Panama
Canal treaties and the Equal Rights Amendment. . . .

Anti-abortion Groups

The big mama of the antiabortion movement is the
National Right to Life Committee, which sponsored last
week's rally in Cincinnati. Organized six years ago, the
N.R.L.C. claims more than 11 million members of 1,800
chapters across the country. The committee hopes to amass
millions of dollars for next year's elections. It has been
spurred into more forceful involvement in politics by com-

petition from several activist groups that are at the front of the fight for a ban on abortions. Among them:

National Pro-Life Political Action Committee. Based in Chicago, this group is headed by Father Charles Fiore, 45, a Dominican priest with a reddish beard and a combative temperament that sometimes offends his superiors. When Father Fiore urged Catholics to stop contributing to any community fund drive benefiting organizations that aid abortions, John Cardinal Cody ordered him to stop preaching in the Chicago archdiocese. One reason: some of the same fund drives also support Catholic charities. Uncowed, Father Fiore asks: "What does it profit an archdiocese if it gains $3.7 million and suffers the loss of its own soul?"

Life Amendment Political Action Committee. Run in Washington by Paul Brown, 41, a soft-spoken former executive of the K mart Corporation, this group is best known to antiabortionists for its hit lists of pro-choice incumbents. Its record of victories is impressive, though its leaders often count among them politicians who were defeated for reasons other than their stands on abortion. Nevertheless, Brown't outfit has been effective as a link between Washington and activists at state and congressional levels who are fighting against abortion. Brown raised $95,000 last year for congressional campaigns and hopes to funnel $250,000 into campaigns next year. He sees the possibility of winning support from 41 Senators for an antiabortion amendment by 1981. Says he: "We would then launch a filibuster, and we would shut down the Government until we got the amendment."

Life Political Action Committee. Unlike Brown's group, this Washington-based organization is primarily an umbrella organization that coordinates the activities of about 30 antiabortion groups in the states. The committee was formed by Lee Edwards, 46, deputy publicity director for Barry Goldwater's presidential campaign in 1964, and Joe Barrett, 42, a former trucking executive who had been a political backer of John and Robert Kennedy. The committee works primarily to influence elections for state legislatures by organizing political action committees at local levels.

Pro-Choice Groups

The zealousness of the pro-life groups stems in part from frustration. Despite their smashing legislative victories, the number of legal abortions in the US has increased steadily, from 899,000 in 1974 to about 1.3 million in 1977. Further, a study by the US Center for Disease Control in Atlanta shows that, despite the Hyde amendment, most low-income women are neither bearing unwanted children nor turning to kitchen-table abortionists. That is because 76% of the poor women seeking abortions live in the 15 populous states that have used state funds to make up for the lost federal money; many of the other 24% can get financial help from private groups or obtain abortions at low-cost clinics.

The pro-choice groups are well aware that they have lost ground to the more active antiabortionists. Admits Karen Mulhauser, executive director of the *National Abortion Rights Action League:* "After the Supreme Court decision, a lot of our groups on the state level folded up. Our people went on to ERA, environmental problems and the like. We relaxed, and the other side began to organize." Based in Washington, her group is spending about $1 million this year in a drive to raise funds, expand its field operations and enlarge membership beyond the present 65,000. It has distributed some 200,000 postcards bearing the message, "I'm pro-choice and I vote."

The league last month enlisted some 100 clergy men and women of various faiths to apply pressure by lobbying members of Congress, hoping to blunt the religious side of the abortion issue, which has long been dominated by the Roman Catholic clergy. Said one rebellious Catholic priest, Father Joseph O'Rourke, who was among the pro-choice lobbyists in Washington: "The antiabortionists are anti-free, antiwomen and anti-Christian."

Some 150 other pro-choice advocates joined the effort. They met vocal opposition from pro-lifers who were picketing Capitol Hill. Two women pushing baby strollers had a curt conversation. "This is a pro-life baby," said one. Replied the other: "This is a pro-choice baby."

The target of much of the lobbying was polite but unbudgeable Congressman Hyde. As members of the clergy clustered about him, Hyde said calmly: "I'm for everyone to follow the dictates of their conscience. But a constitutional right to want something doesn't mean the right to have the Government pay for it." As the debate warmed up, Hyde tossed out one of his favorite lines: "There are one million children who are thrown away like Kleenex because someone thinks that they are not as valuable as a snail darter." Hyde brushed aside all counterarguments. "Taking a human life with the taxpayers' money is abhorrent," he said, "and I intend to use the political process to stop it."

The visiting churchmen and women walked away, frustrated and angry at their inability to make any headway with Hyde. "He's intractable," observed Patricia Gavett, national director of the *Religious Coalition for Abortion Rights*. "But I think he turned our clergy on politically." The aroused ministers quickly discovered that the politics of abortion is a bruising business. Last week a more stringent version of the Hyde amendment easily passed the House. It would ban federal funds for all abortions except cases in which a woman's life is in danger. As in past years, the Senate is expected to add exceptions for cases of rape, incest or potentially severe damage to the mother's physical health and then pass the legislation handily. [A compromise bill was passed in October 1979, temporarily providing funds in certain cases.—Ed.]

OF ABORTION AND THE UNFAIRNESS OF LIFE [2]

"Life is unfair," John Kennedy observed at a press conference one day in 1962. The thought had a certain stoic

[2] Essay by Lance Morrow, senior writer. *Time.* v 110, no 5, p 49. Ag. 1, '77. Reprinted by permission from TIME, The Weekly Newsmagazine; Copyright Time Inc. 1977.

grace about it: its truth was brutally confirmed the following year in Dallas. Life *is* unfair. Kennedy was talking about citizens' military obligations, about the restive Army reservists who were being held on active duty even after the Berlin crisis had subsided. Now Jimmy Carter has brought up the unfairness doctrine to explain his policy on abortion. Somehow the dictum comes out this time with a mean-spirited edge, like something from the lips of Dickens' Mr. Podsnap.

Abortion, of course, is a painful issue that has given rise to few ennobling ideas. Anyone who comes to an easy decision on the subject is probably a moral idiot. Four years ago [1973], the Supreme Court declared it legal to terminate a pregnancy in the first three months, or up to six months in some circumstances. About a million legal abortions are now performed every year in the US—a third of them paid for with Medicaid funds. But last month the Supreme Court decided, by a vote of 6 to 3, that the states and localities are free, if they wish, to deny Medicaid money for abortions. Both houses of Congress have made their contribution by passing provisions that forbid federal Medicaid payments for abortions, although the measures differ in severity.

In other words, abortions are fine for the women who, on the whole, have the least pressing need for them: women at least well enough off to buy their own way out of their fecundity. The women (often young girls) who cannot raise the money must presumably either bear their unwanted children—thus bringing many thousands of new customers to welfare—or find some way, however dangerous, dark and filthy, to kill the fetus more cheaply. Such methods have had the result of sometimes disposing of the mother as well.

When he was asked at a press conference about the logic of this, the President took up John Kennedy's line. "Well," said Carter, "as you know, there are many things in life that are not fair, that wealthy people can afford and poor people can't." Anatole France in the last century appraised that kind of elegant fatalism: "The law in its majesty equality forbids the rich as well as the poor to sleep under bridges."

Certainly a principal purpose of human government must be to mitigate the unfairness that seems to be an integral part of human life—or, at the very least, not to compound it. The judicial system is meant to mediate, to knock the chaos of human behavior into a manageable pattern. The goal of fairness underlies American education, which has been regarded, sometimes more hopefully than accurately, as the way to give everyone an equal chance. Medicaid was meant to provide fairness in health care, so that if a poor man needs an $800 appendectomy or a $15,000 coronary bypass, he will, in theory, receive something like the same treatment as a character who arrives at the hospital by *grossen* Mercedes.

Some people believe, of course, that government has gone entirely too far in trying to make life fairer. The formula of best government equaling least government has vanished into the vast bureaucratic software that produces welfare, food stamps and unemployment benefits. But if government is indeed, for better or worse, promoting the health, education and welfare of the American people, why should federal help for those who seek abortions be excluded?

One answer is that abortion is morally wrong—even, some say, a blithely conducted form of infanticide. There are painfully compelling reasons to oppose abortion; philosophers and theologians have done so for many centuries. The Hippocratic Oath includes a stricture against aiding an abortion. (Many medical schools now use a rephrased version of the oath to circumvent the abortion issue.) The procedure involves the destruction of a form of human life—life *in utero,* but life nonetheless. By the sixth week, almost all of the human organs are in place; by the eighth, brain-wave activity can be detected. The right-to-life lobby displays pictures of those tiny hands and feet, those grisly fetuses pickled in jars; but bad taste does not disable their argument.

The other reality is just as disturbing. Without legal and affordable abortion, many lives in progress are hopelessly ruined; the unwanted children very often grow up unloved, battered, conscienceless, trapped and criminal. A whole new virus of misery breeds in the accidental zygotes.

Both technically and morally, the most difficult problem is to decide at what precise instant life occurs. Is it in the actual conceptive collision of sperm and egg? Is it only when the fetus "quickens," at five months or so? The Supreme Court in 1973 simply said that abortion in the early stages of pregnancy should be a medical, not a criminal matter; it was best left to the judgment of the woman and her physician. Given the violence of warring moralities in the abortion debate, the law was unreasonably strained. The statutes forbidding abortion were a kind of Volstead Act, so widely (and often dangerously) violated as to be worse than useless. The court was therefore wise to send the question back to the privacy of individual consciences. The many who believe abortion morally wrong should honor their convictions. But the dilemma is too difficult to permit anti-abortionists to impose their beliefs, no matter how deeply held, upon people who disagree.

What then of public financing for abortions? Should citizens have to pay for an operation they find morally repugnant? A few years ago, stores sold a nihilistically spirited black box: when one pushed a button on its side, the box whirred and opened, a hand appeared from under a lid—and turned the box off. The Supreme Court's latest decision—and Carter's attitude toward it—has something of the same self-canceling effect. The court made abortion legal; now it has rescinded an important advantage of that legality by making it hard for the poor to obtain abortions. On narrow constitutional grounds, the court does have a point; states and communities should have the right to decide how to spend their tax money. But the refusal to spend it creates a new configuration marked by inconsistency and hypocrisy.

Carter did not contribute much with his reflections on

how unfair the human condition is. Everyone knows that life is unfair. It is also, as Thomas Hobbes pointed out, "solitary, poor, nasty, brutish and short." Life's unfairness is so self-evident in, say, slums, or institutions for the retarded and insane, or in any cancer ward, that it needs no sad-but-true sighings from the White House. To be sure, the President did have other reasons; he fears, for one thing, that abortion may become merely belated contraception. Certainly, responsible people should take greater care to practice contraception in the first place. And surely it is too casual to say, as Psychiatrist Thomas Szasz has said, that abortion "should be available [in the first two or three months] in the same way as, say, an operation for the beautification of a nose." Besides, pregnancy is not a disease, except in a metaphorical sense, for those whose lives are blighted by it.

So Carter is correct in suggesting that abortion involves unique moral questions outside the simple rationale for Medicaid payments. Still, the ultimate morality or immorality of it need not be decided in order to judge the principle of fairness. The undoubted risks of making abortion too easily available are outweighed by the risks of making it too difficult or impossible to obtain. Since the only intelligent argument to be made for abortion is that it is a social necessity, fairness and logic dictate that it must be available especially to those who, wanting it, cannot afford it. To say that abortion, while legal, is immoral but that only the poor shall be saved from this immorality by a fastidious government is not only unfair but absurd.

THE WRONG DECISION [3]

How one feels about the U.S. Supreme Court decision removing the legal restrictions on early abortions may well

[3] Editorial from the Birmingham (Alabama) *News.* Ja. 28, '73. Title supplied by the editor. Reprinted by permission of The *News.*

depend on a number of factors—whether one is male or female, old or young, married or single, religiously oriented or agnostic, or whether one is pregnant or not pregnant.

Since nearly all English-American law is based in moral and ethical assumptions, it is difficult as a practical matter for a court to come down in support of one moral assumption without abusing one or more concepts in another area.

In the case of abortions, the Supreme Court decision apparently sought to walk the fence between two moral-legal issues.

The decision, in essence, said it is more moral to preserve the individual female's right to decide whether or not to terminate a pregnancy, at least for the first 12 weeks. At that point and for the next 12 weeks the court said it is more moral for the state to obligate itself to see that a pregnancy is terminated only within the limits of certain medical standards. In the last 12 weeks the court, in effect, abandoned support of the individual mother's rights, and opted for the moral right of the unborn child to life.

At issue in the court's mind was "when does a fetus become a human being?"

By virtue of its ruling, the court said, in essence, that the fetus is not a human being up to the point at which it cannot "live"—maintain its own vital functions—separated from the mother. Or, the fetus becomes a human being at that point at which it *can* maintain its vital functions separated from the mother.

The question is one that religious thinkers and medical men have pondered for centuries without being able to resolve definitively.

Historically the Judeo-Christian traditions have stood solidly aligned against abortion except in rare cases.

At the center of both Judaism and Christianity and many other religions is the concept of the sacred worth of the person and that the person's life begins at conception.

The religious understanding is that since man has not the power to create life, he has no right to end it. Since God is the only giver of life, the taking of life must also be His prerogative only. For men to take or end a life is to subvert the will of God.

Some ethicists in the biological sciences say that modern genetics tend to confirm the religious view. The genetic code, they say, seems to affirm that a person was *from the point of conception* what he essentially becomes in every cell.

Regardless of their faith, up until recent years most doctors refused categorically to implement abortions unless the life of the mother was unquestionably in jeopardy as a result of pregnancy.

In the last several decades the interpretation of the mother's jeopardy has been liberalized to include her mental and emotional health. Concurrent with this liberalization has been a tendency to look ahead to consider if circumstances are such that the child can be properly cared for.

Lifting the legal barriers to abortion during the first three months of pregnancy has by no means resolved the religious-moral issue. The debate is likely to continue far into the future.

The issue has simply been left up to the individual, her conscience and the position of the particular religious tradition to which the individual subscribes.

With the legal restrictions removed, it will be desirable, if not imperative, that the religious-moral considerations be brought to bear to help the parents, wed or not, as well as doctors to make as responsible decisions as possible.

As for the propriety of the court's decision, we will have to agree with the minority opinion.

Justice William H. Rehnquist properly challenged the validity of the opinion when he wrote: "The decision here to break the term of pregnancy into three distinct terms and to outline the permissible restrictions the state may impose in each one, for example, partakes more of judicial legislation than it does of a determination of the intent of the drafters of the 14th Amendment."

And Justice Byron R. White was essentially right in judging the decision an exercise of "raw judicial power" and in finding that the court has scarcely any "reason or authority for its action."

Not being able to see into the future, but suspecting that vast changes in society and the human condition will take place in the next 25 to 100 years, it is completely possible that the decision will be invalidated sooner than anyone expects.

But in the meantime, great social changes as a result of the decision are unlikely. It is doubtful that even the quality of this area of life will be more than peripherally affected. For despite feeble attempts to abrogate it, the Judeo-Christian ethic is deeply ingrained in the American character and not likely to be erased in the foreseeable future.

And there is further assurance in recognizing that mankind's moral attitude toward abortion was ancient even centuries before the issue became a matter of law.

AFFIRMING THE RIGHT TO DECIDE [4]

The Supreme Court's sweeping decision which in effect has struck down the repressive or restrictive abortion statutes which until now have prevailed in all but a handful of states is remarkable for its common sense, its humaneness and most of all its affirmation of an individual's right to privacy.

This is a ruling of which the high court may be justly proud, for it met straight on and dealt comprehensibly with an emotional issue—indeed in many places a political issue as well—that it might easily have ducked or skirted. And it is of more than passing significance that the majority opinion for the 7-to-2 decision was written by Justice [Harry A.] Blackmun, a "strict constructionist" appointee of President Nixon who has not hesitated to exploit the abortion controversy for partisan purposes.

[4] Editorial from the St. Louis *Post-Dispatch*. Ja. 28, '73. Title supplied by the editor. Reprinted by permission from the newspaper.

The essential facts of the ruling, which dealt with laws in Texas and Georgia, may be quickly summarized: states may not interfere with a woman's right to a medical abortion in the first six months of pregnancy, although after the first trimester a state may regulate abortion procedures in ways to promote "maternal health"; in the last three months of pregnancy when the fetus may be viable, states may prohibit abortions unless they are necessary to preserve a woman's life or health and, finally, residency requirements which restrict the rights of pregnant women to use medical facilities are unconstitutional.

Thus the legal arguments against abortion have been thoroughly disposed of. The responsible course now for state legislatures, including those of Missouri and Illinois, will be to resist efforts to circumvent the intent of the court's decision through the passage of legislation that would place any obstacle in the way of those who either need or desire abortions.

Explicit in Justice Blackmun's opinion is the overriding principle that abortions are a matter to be decided by medical judgment, that states have no more right to prohibit abortions in the first six months of pregnancy than they have to prohibit, say, tonsillectomies. The court decisively rejected the notion that the fetus has constitutional rights by pointing out "the unborn have never been recognized in the law as person (s) ," and it sensibly declined to become entangled in the argument of when life begins. Inasmuch as "those trained in . . . medicine, philosophy and theology are unable to arrive at any consensus," Justice Blackmun wrote, the judiciary is scarcely in a position to speculate on the subject.

The decision is a compassionate one because it recognizes that an unwanted pregnancy may be far more harmful in terms of mental stress and the physical toil of childbearing than an abortion. This harm is particularly severe in the case of unmarried women, who must bear the stigma of having fatherless children. It is compassionate, too, in that abortions now will be far easier to obtain by the poor, who in states such as Missouri have had no option other than continuing an unwanted pregnancy or being subjected to the mortal risks of the back alley abortionist.

But if the legal barriers to abortions have been almost totally removed, the moral questions pertaining to the procedure remain. And so they should. No one ought to interpret the court's action as a signal for state or national laws encouraging abortions. The question of whether to terminate a pregnancy must be a private one to answer; it is a decision that inevitably must involve a person's deepest moral values, whether they be inspired by religious beliefs or drawn from secular teachings or experience.

What the court has done is give women the right to make this decision; and that is what the right to privacy is all about. It is the right to be free from state interference in reaching purely personal decisions.

CHANGING VIEWS OF ABORTION [5]

Nearly five years after the Supreme Court decision made it legal, abortion continues to be a hot issue. Everybody and their mothers have an opinion, but it's not always possible to predict who is on which side of the fence just by knowing some of their more apparent characteristics such as age, ethnicity, socioeconomic status or even religion.

One reason for this uncertainty is that Americans, individually or in identity groups, seem to be constantly reevaluating their stand; and another, according to Theodore C. Wagenaar, PhD, and Ingeborg W. Knol of Miami University in Oxford, Ohio, is that all those more obvious characteristics don't explain much about why people feel as they do. In a study using National Opinion Research Center data for the years 1973 and 1975. Wagenaar and Knol say that the 15 common variables they looked at to-

[5] Article in *Human Behavior*. v 7, no 3, p 58. Mr. '78. Copyright © 1978 *Human Behavior* Magazine. Reprinted by permission.

gether could not account for even a quarter of the differences in people's opinions on the issue of abortion.

Hard and Soft Reasons

Subjects, some 1,500 randomly selected Americans for each of the two survey years, were asked their opinion about the possibility of a legal abortion for a woman in six different situations: when her chances of having a seriously defective child are great; when she could be endangered by the pregnancy; when she was pregnant because of rape; when she was married but did not want any more children; when she was poor and could not afford any more children; or when she was single and did not want to marry the baby's father. The researchers report that overall, and for both years of the study, over 80 percent of Americans okayed abortion for one of the first three "hard" reasons, and over 40 percent gave their support in the latter three "soft" cases.

Beyond that, however, there were subtle shifts in approval and disapproval from 1973 to 1975, such that women became slightly more supportive and men a little more antagonistic; blacks grew more favoring while whites became somewhat less so; Catholics, while remaining the most disapproving of the religious groups, became slightly more supportive in the face of a slight conservative streak among non-Catholics. The more rapid increase of support among these formerly, and still largely, nonsupportive groups "may reflect a catching up with the types of persons who more readily supported abortion—the more highly educated, northeasterners, westerners, whites and those without a religion," suggest Wagenaar and Knol.

The composite picture is still someone with these characteristics but who is also higher in economic status or has been unemployed in the past 10 years and has minimal exposure to children. In general, age, sex, marital status, political affiliation, city size and receipt of government aid had nothing to do with a person's views on abortion.

"Perhaps various psychological and life-experience variables may prove to be more salient than the usual demographic variables," Wagenaar and Knol conclude.

THE FIRST "TEST-TUBE" BABY [6]

She was a world-wide celebrity even before she was born, and now at the age of two months Louise Brown remains at the center of a storm of scientific excitement and controversy. For the blue-eyed, blond infant, whose gusty screams kept a whole nursery of babies awake a few hours after her birth, is the first child ever conceived outside her mother's womb.

The arrival of test-tube baby Louise in the drab British mill town of Oldham was greeted by a mixture of awe, hope, and fear. Researchers applauded the medical success of Dr. Patrick Steptoe and Dr. Robert Edwards, the gynecologist and physiologist who actually created Louise in the laboratory. Thousands of infertile women drew inspiration from the successfully completed pregnancy of a woman whom doctors had declared totally unable ever to bear her own child.

On the other hand, philosophers and ethicists issued grim warnings that the miracle of Louise Brown's birth indicated the arrival of medicine at the brave new world of asexual procreation forecast more than half a century ago by novelist Aldous Huxley.

Many foresaw, too, that the achievement would undoubtedly presage such abhorrent developments as surrogate mothers, completely artificial wombs, and further tampering with the evolution of the human race.

Such forebodings were far from the minds of John and Lesley Brown, a young couple from the British port city

[6] Article entitled "A Happy Accident? More Test-tube Babies?" by Peter Gwynne, science editor, Newsweek. Science Digest. v 84, no 4, p 7-12. O. '78. Reprinted by permission from SCIENCE DIGEST. Copyright 1978. The Hearst Corporation. ALL RIGHTS RESERVED.

of Bristol, when they first visited Dr. Steptoe two years ago. Lesley Brown is one of the roughly two percent of married women whose fallopian tubes are blocked. Since the tubes are the channels through which sperm travel to fertilize the mother's eggs and the fertilized eggs make their way to the uterus, the condition precludes normal conception.

The blockages can sometimes be repaired by surgery, but Lesley Brown did not respond to that type of treatment. Thus, when a two-year wait to adopt a child turned out fruitlessly, the couple decided to consult with Dr. Steptoe, who had been collaborating with Dr. Edwards on test-tube conception experiments since 1966.

The Brown's chances of conceiving a healthy baby seemed small even then. For while Drs. Steptoe and Edwards had shown that they could mate human sperm and eggs in the test-tube, and even reimplant the fertilized egg inside the mothers, none of the roughly 80 pregnancies that they had induced in that way had lasted more than a few weeks. In every case, the fetus was aborted spontaneously. But the two researchers were continually altering their techniques, and in this case a new scientific approach worked.

Lesley Brown was under Dr. Steptoe's care for more than a year prior to the conception of Louise. Late in 1976, the gynecologist removed his patient's diseased fallopian tubes entirely, removing any faint hope that she could ever conceive naturally, but giving him a much better view of her ovaries.

The Procedure

Then on November 10 [1977], using a self-lit probe called a laparoscope whose use he had pioneered, Dr. Steptoe plucked a ripening egg from one of Lesley Brown's ovaries and passed it on to Dr. Edwards.

The physiologist, who had traveled 175 miles from Cambridge University to Oldham for the event, then mixed the egg with sperm from John Brown in a cylindrical glass vessel, and watched as one of the sperm fertilized the egg. Dr. Edwards then transferred the fertilized egg to a special nutrient solution which he had devised over more than a decade of experimentation, and monitored it as it split into two, four, and finally eight cells.

In the past, Drs. Edwards and Steptoe had allowed the fertilized eggs to continue dividing in the test-tube for four or five days until they reached the 64-cell stage. But this time, convinced that the egg could be reintroduced safely into the body, Steptoe reimplanted it after just two and a half days in the laboratory, inserting it in Lesley Brown's uterus with a tube that passed through her cervix.

Shortly afterwards, tests indicated that the fertilized egg had attached itself to Mrs. Brown's uterine wall—and this time, unlike previous tries with other would-be mothers, the pregnancy continued for weeks and then months.

Lesley Brown and her growing fetus were monitored with extraordinary care, using such techniques as amniocentesis and ultrasound, and she was admitted to the Oldham General Hospital two months before Louise was expected. Nine days before the due date, the mother-to-be developed toxemia—an increase in blood pressure that could harm her unborn child.

Dr. Steptoe decided to operate, and delivered Louise, a five-pound, 12-ounce baby.

"The last time I saw her, she was just eight cells in a test-tube," said Dr. Edwards. "She was beautiful then, and she's still beautiful now!"

But behind the beauty lurks the beast—in the form of nightmares in the minds of theologians, ethicists, and philosophers. Three types of concerns exist regarding Louise Brown's unique and astonishing method of conception. They involve short-, medium-, and long-term worries.

One immediate problem is that thousands of infertile women have gained new hope of bearing a child from the first breathless accounts of Louise's birth.

Unfortunately for those hopes, they cannot be satisfied for more than a minuscule proportion of infertile women even in the best of circumstances.

Unavailing Efforts

Very few medical teams around the world possess anywhere near the extraordinary medical skills of Drs. Steptoe and Edwards in their controversial field. And the facts are that even those two men needed a dozen years to hone their skills, and they tried their procedure more than four score times before they produced a test-tube conception that resulted in a successful birth.

The two researchers emphasize that they still regard their procedure as experimental.

The health of Louise herself is not entirely guaranteed. For while the child undoubtedly is free of gross physical and mental defects, she cannot be considered necessarily free of minor problems as she becomes older.

For the moment, however, the greatest risk to Louise Brown's health appears to be that of excessive time in the limelight.

More to Come?

Given her unique and pioneering mode of conception, she always will be a focus of attention.

The obvious solution to this nagging problem, as Dr. Steptoe points out, is to produce more test-tube babies, thus diminishing Louise's rarity value. Drs. Steptoe and Edwards report pregnancies induced in several other women since Louise was conceived, and a group at St. Thomas' Hospital in London reimplanted a fertilized egg in a hopeful mother-to-be within a day of Louise's birth. But none of the implants come with an iron-clad guarantee of success.

Fundamentally, medical researchers are worried that Drs. Steptoe and Edwards managed to produce Louise more by chance than design—that they somehow hit on a combination of circumstances that neither they nor any other research group will be able to repeat.

"What we don't know," said one member of the St. Thomas' team, "is whether Dr. Steptoe has been able to overcome the basic problems of test-tube conception, or whether Mr. and Mrs. Brown's baby must be put down to good luck."

An ever greater fear exists: That the baby's good health is also a matter of lucky chance, and that future test-tube children might be genetically or physically less than perfect at birth.

"The greatest tragedy," warns Dr. Luigi Mastroianni of the University of Pennsylvania, "would be to treat an infertile woman in this way and present her with a baby that was malformed."

Many Stages Skipped

The basis for Dr. Mastroianni's concern is that the two British researchers skipped many of the stages normally regarded as essential in the application of new medical technology to humans. Usually, scientists first try out new procedures on lower animals, such as mice or rats; next they apply it to higher creatures such as dogs; then they perfect it on monkeys or other primates before finally using the technique on people.

Heart transplants, for example, were developed in just this way. But before Louise Brown's birth, only three species had been conceived in the test-tube, reimplanted in the mother's body, and successfully brought to term—rats, mice, and rabbits.

The immediate concerns should be answered soon enough, by either the successful deliveries of a number of test-tube babies or the failure to produce healthy children. If the whole procedure really does work well, experts in ethics will be able to examine some of the medium-term dilemmas.

The most imponderable undoubtedly will be that of the legal status of fertilized eggs before reimplantation. That won't just involve simply dry legalistic debates, because it will be literally a life-and-death matter. Its resolution will decide whether scientists can simply throw used or defective fertilized eggs down the drain or whether they will have to resort to heroic measures to keep them alive.

Plainly, fertilized eggs are different from human fetuses inside the womb. While fetuses can threaten their mothers' well-being, fertilized eggs in the test-tube threaten no one, and impinge on nobody's rights. Thus, few lawyers would argue that they can be disposed of according to legally established principles of abortion. Yet discarding fertilized eggs almost certainly will become an issue, because hormone treatments prior to the extraction of eggs from would-be mothers of test-tube babies inevitably will produce more eggs than necessary, thus giving doctors the opportunity to select the "best-looking" fertilized egg for reimplantation.

Some of the rejects would have obvious defects. But others may stand to lose their chance of life because they happen to be the "wrong sex."

"Will the right to life of these entities be just a matter between a doctor and his plumber?" muses one ethicist rhetorically.

One's natural horror at the idea of throwing proto-humans away with the garbage must be mitigated by one startling fact: Only a third of all the eggs that are fertilized inside the bodies of women actually survive as far as birth. Most are aborted spontaneously within a month or two after fertilization.

Nature plainly has its own flushing-out process. But should man institute the same procedure when he takes over control of procreation?

This part of the debate obviously focuses on a fundamental question: When does human life really begin? Does it start at the exact moment that the father's sperm penetrates the mother's egg? Or does it, perhaps, only become viable when the fertilized egg implants itself solidly in the mother's uterus? Does life begin even later inside the womb? Or is the beginning of individual human existence a nebulous process that has no sharp, specific starting point?

One ethical nightmare is surrogate mothers—women who would rent out their wombs to carry to term the test-tube induced fetuses of, say, rich women or movie stars who have neither time nor inclination to go through pregnancy.

Beyond that is an even grimmer specter: The development of artificial wombs that would allow children to be conceived, carried, and born without any human contact. A group at Johns Hopkins University headed by Dr. Yu-Chih Hsu already has managed to preserve embryo mice in the test-tube almost halfway through their normal period of gestation, and other teams have developed artificial wombs in which they can sustain premature lambs that would otherwise die.

One Remaining Step

Eventually, the two techniques could combine to produce motherless gestation—although Dr. Hsu expresses his hope that such technology never will be applied to humans. "It raises too many ethical questions," he says.

But if fully artificial wombs for humans do become possible, only one more small step would remain to be taken toward the completely man-made society that Huxley forecast in *Brave New World,* replete with genetically designed geniuses and morons.

That step is genetic tampering with the just-fertilized eggs to produce the desired qualities in the baby-to-be. With the emergence of such techniques as recombinant DNA technology—which allows scientists to replace individual genes—such tampering does not seem unduly futuristic. At that point, scientists would have to face the ultimate moral questions posed by Father Richard McCormick of the Kennedy Institute of Ethics at Georgetown University:

"What qualities are to be bred in, what defects to be screened out?" he asks. "What constitutes the 'desirable human being'? And who decides this?"

A Ban Is Unlikely

For all the theological and moral doubts, the fact is that test-tube baby technology has arrived, and scientific history suggests it is unlikely that its application can be banned.

"I take the position that if we have the technology it will be used," said a University of Virginia law professor, Walter Wadlington, at a recent hearing of a House of Representatives Committee on a proposal to end a moratorium on test-tube baby research in this country.

The hopeful side of the story is that scientists (and the public) are aware of the gruesome implications of their work, and thus in a strong position to prevent its worst imaginable excesses from happening.

AN ALTERNATIVE ROUTE TO PARENTHOOD [7]

The mere mention of "test-tube babies" triggers instant repugnance in most of us. Visions arise, from Aldous Huxley's *Brave New World*, of moving assembly lines of glassware out of which babies are decanted at each terminus by a detached and impersonal technician. Procreation thus becomes reproduction in the full factorylike connotation of that word. And as we conjure up the distasteful (at the least) scene, words like *mechanization* and *dehumanization* reverberate through our neuronal networks.

Nevertheless, despite the offense to our sensibilities provoked by even the thought of artificial wombs, there is a valid case to be made for test-tube babies in the full Huxleyan image—not mass-produced on an assembly line, perhaps, but nevertheless wholly and "artificially" grown in a scientifically monitored environment without ever being carried in the uterus of a human mother. Such a case can be made (which does not mean that I personally advocate it) on the basis not merely of bizarre and exotic specula-

[7] "Science Letter" entitled "The Case for Test-Tube Babies," by Albert Rosenfeld, senior editor. *Saturday Review.* v 5, no 27, p 10-14. O. 28, '78, © Saturday Review, 1978. All rights reserved. Reprinted by permission.

tions but of purely humane, down-to-earth considerations having to do with the health of individual babies.

As reproductive biologists proceed with further research on animals, there should be sufficient time (if we don't waste it) to continue thinking about and debating the essential questions: whether or not we wish to utilize these biotechnologies for the creation of human beings, and if so, for what purposes. The ethical implications are profound and far-reaching, and each of us should make a contribution to the final decisions. Let us not proceed the way we have until now—letting each banner headline provoke us into a spate of concern that dissipates as soon as the event-of-the-moment has passed.

The test tube is, of course, the symbolic, not the actual, container employed in the world of *in vitro* procreation. *In vitro* means "in glass," though the laboratory container or device may be plastic, ceramic, metal, or any combination of materials, of any shape, size, or complexity. The common theme is that babies are created—or started on their way—outside the human body, by means that bypass the conventional sexual channels. Though the offspring of artificial insemination (AI) are loosely referred to as test-tube babies, the "test tube" in this instance holds only the sperm—which is not usually contributed by the husband of the prospective mother, but more often by an anonymous donor selected by the doctor. In some cases, the sperm is taken from deep-frozen storage.

Types of Artificial Insemination

Tens of thousands of babies are estimated to be born each year in the U.S. via AID (artificial insemination, donor; in contrast to AIH—artificial insemination, husband). Our present population probably includes more than 100,000 test-tube adults, indistinguishable from anyone else, who were conceived by AID. Exact numbers of AI births are hard to come by, since the technique's legal status still hovers in a fuzz of ambiguities and the method of conception is not always recorded on the birth certificate.

But the practice is so widespread, and has been with us for such a long time, that we have obviously made our uneasy *de facto* peace with at least this type of test-tube baby.

In artificial insemination, when fertilization occurs, it does so in the usual manner, in one of the fallopian tubes of the would-be mother. The kind of test-tube baby recently making international headlines, however, entails *in vitro* fertilization. The radical difference between AI and this method is that, with *in vitro* fertilization, the egg is removed from the woman's body—usually because the tubes leading from ovary to uterus are blocked. Insemination (in this case usually with the husband's sperm) and conception both take place *in vitro*. Only after the egg is fertilized and has, after several days, divided repeatedly to become a cluster of cells called the blastocyst, is the incipient embryo transferred back into the woman, where it will implant itself into the wall of her hormone-prepared uterus in a normal manner.

The issues about test-tube babies are not new; what has made them controversial today is the fact that they have resurfaced with new credibility, and therefore with greater intensity, because of the historic birth in Britain. This event was ironically juxtaposed in the news with a lawsuit in New York brought by the couple who might themselves have become the parents of the world's first test-tube baby six years earlier. In 1972 Dr. Landrum Shettles, of the Columbia-Presbyterian Medical Center in New York, removed an egg from a Florida woman, Doris Del Zio, and fertilized it *in vitro* with her husband's sperm—much as Drs. Patrick Steptoe and Robert Edwards were to do with Lesley Brown and her husband in 1978, when the state of the art was considerably more advanced. But Shettles's experiment was aborted—in both its meanings—when his superior, Dr. Raymond Vande Wiele, destroyed it. Perhaps Vande Wiele was indignant that Shettles was "playing God" in this fashion; but in the view of the Del Zios, it was Vande Wiele himself who was playing God by destroying their potential baby. Surprisingly, Mrs. Del Zio was awarded $50,000 in damages (she was suing for a million and a half), which suggests that the jurors were at least convinced that the "test-tube" attempt was neither preposterous nor immoral.

My purpose is not to repeat all the details of this by-now-familiar story, nor the ethical arguments pro and con; I want to proceed directly to the topic of the ultimate test-tube baby, à la Huxley—the all-the-way *in vitro* baby, conceived *in vitro* and brought through all its embryonic and fetal stages *in vitro* to its full-term birth or "decantation." This is not to say that the bioengineering knowhow for this feat is anywhere in sight, yet there seems little doubt that it could be accomplished—and probably sooner than most people think—if anyone were sufficiently motivated to bring it about. But why would anyone want to?

Offsetting Birth Defects

For one thing, more than 200,000 babies with birth defects are born in the United States every year. Of these defects, probably not more than one in five is purely genetic in origin; the others are largely congenital in nature, the result of something gone wrong during a critical stage of development. It has been argued that, if the potential baby could be visible during the whole of its development—in its "womb with a view," as it were—and its growth monitored daily in detail, hundreds of thousands of birth defects might be averted. The embryo-fetus, which has always been on its own in its dark isolation ward for the nine-month-long prenatal period, could thus become as accessible to medical intervention as any other ailing patient.

An expectant mother or father who has a known risk of a serious congenital defect, or a woman who has experienced repeated miscarriages, might well elect to use *in vitro* methods if given reasonable assurance of a better chance for a healthy, full-term baby. A Louis Harris poll made in 1969 for *Life* magazine suggested that many people who at first had expressed horror at test-tube births would find such biotechnologies quite acceptable under these circumstances.

A Controlled Environment

Apart from the advantage of preventing birth defects through early intervention, it may well turn out that the fetus's mere presence in a controlled and protected environment might in itself offer preventive insurance. In that case, the methods could become more attractive to prospective parents who do *not* have a family history of birth defects. It does look more and more as if a mother's womb is perhaps *not* the safest possible place in the world for a delicately developing being to spend the first nine months of its life. Year by year we learn of yet additional hazards of life *in utero:* of the dangers, for instance, of retarded development or malformations due to viral infections, like rubella, that the mother may have contracted, or drugs she may be taking, or X-rays to which she may have been exposed. And of dangers from the mother's personal habits —excessive smoking or drinking, for example—or even from extreme emotional disturbances or depressions that could change her biochemistry in ways disadvantageous to the developing child.

Suppose the expectant father is a wife-beater? The fetus could become a "battered child" prenatally. What of all the other accidents and hazards that might befall the fetus's highly mobile human carrier? What if the mother has other handicaps—is severely diabetic, grossly obese, under-age or over-age? If the mother is improperly nourished, through poverty, ignorance, or carelessness, the fetus too will be malnourished and perhaps developmentally retarded or even brain-damaged; or if the fetus proceeds to a relatively normal, full-term birth, it may still be a "low birth-weight," and therefore a high-risk, baby.

All in all, one can begin to see the possible advantages of a developing fetus's being nourished and nurtured in an environment, "artificial" though it be, that is more protected. Now, of course, it may turn out that the fetus *needs* some of the jostling that goes with being carried by a human mother, needs some of the noises it hears—the mother's heartbeat, for instance—as well as other distractions that may provide a kind of early sensory training for later exposure to the outside world. So it may be necessary to impart the requisite jostling or rocking motions to the artificial womb, to pipe in the recorded sound of a mother's heartbeat (as is now sometimes done for premature infants undergoing neonatal intensive care), and to simulate other features of the human uterine environment.

Still, assuming the safe availability of this technology, one can imagine not only protecting the fetus from harmful substances and circumstances through monitoring, surveillance, and active medical intervention but also imparting to it some positive benefits. *In vitro* procreation could conceivably increase immunity to a more varied set of hazards; it could also bestow on the child an acquired prenatal tolerance to certain types of tissue that could later be grafted or transplanted without being rejected. Fetal surgery, too, could be performed. Already, in primate centers, monkey fetuses have been removed from the wombs of their mothers—though still remaining attached via the umbilical cord—and, after surgery, replaced in their mothers and allowed to proceed to normal birth.

Questions of Parental Attitudes

Could parents love a child raised in these "unnatural" circumstances, not carried in the mother's body? There is no good reason why not. Adoptive parents seem perfectly capable of unlimited love for children to whom they are in no way related biologically. Should *in vitro* parents love their own genetic progeny any less? Besides, if the expectant parents could visit the *in vitro* facilities with some frequency and regularity during fetal development, if they could *see* their vulnerable offspring at various stages en route to its full-fledged babyhood, they might become attached to it and attentive to its welfare at a much earlier stage. They might begin to feel like parents in advance and thus be better prepared psychologically to take over the actual responsibilities of caring for the baby after its decantation—an occasion for which they could presumably be on hand. But what of the possibly adverse psychological effects on the child of such a birth into the world? Again, much could be learned from careful psychological studies of primates reproduced *in vitro,* just as Dr. Harry Harlow's classic experiments at the University of Wisconsin taught us so much about the future fate of love-deprived baby monkeys.

Relationship to Abortion

When the discussion of such topics as *in vitro* babies arises—at bioethics seminars and workshops, for example—the assumption is usually made that pro-life (anti-abortion) advocates would be inflexibly opposed to any such practices. Yet this may not always and invariably be so. For one thing, there could hardly be any more powerful anti-abortion propaganda than merely the opportunity to *watch* a human fetus develop. Anyone who remembers the beautiful color photographs taken by Lennart Nilsson (or, for that matter, those of Dr. Shettles), which show the fetus at various stages of development—especially those that portray the tiny creature with all parts already clearly recognizable and a thumb stuck in its mouth—knows how hard it is to think of these fetuses as *things,* as mere blobs of protoplasm. They look like babies. And the same perception will have even greater impact when expectant parents observe their own live, wriggling fetuses. Abortion under such conditions would perhaps be undertaken much less casually.

There is yet another reason why those who oppose abortion might favor the development of *in vitro* technology. The central political issue in abortion is after all whether, on the one hand, the life of a fetus can be terminated, and whether, on the other, a woman can be forced—against her will and desire—to become a mother. The "enforced motherhood" objection could be readily resolved if the fetus could be removed from the womb and placed into an *in vitro* environment to complete its gestation. Who would then be responsible for the baby? The state, perhaps?

These issues are by no means academic. Precisely such knotty dilemmas have recently arisen in medical, legal, and bioethical circles in considering what policy to pursue in those instances when a fetus, intended for abortion, is born alive instead. Should it be given to the mother—who didn't want it, though she may now be ready to accept it? Should it perhaps be allowed to die—or, at least, should special efforts to keep it alive be withheld—inasmuch as no one (not the parents and doctors, at any rate) wanted it to live? Is it not entitled to the same intensive-care treatment that would be accorded any other premature infant, regardless of parental intent? And in that case should the state take over the baby as its ward? The California state legislature considered a bill advocating exactly this course.

In most cases such fetuses could not become viable because the technology does not yet exist that can carry them safely through to term. But if a chamber with full life-support systems were at hand, many more fetuses could survive to become babies.

In vitro gestation does not, of course, have to begin at the very beginning, with fertilization. A couple could decide to conceive their baby by sexual intercourse, then have the miniature embryo transferred from its mother to the artificial womb. One of the fears frequently expressed is that many people might choose to use *in vitro* methods for trivial reasons—that is, for mere convenience rather than out of any consideration for the life or health of the fetus.

Research with Animals

Obviously all these ruminations are made at a time when we are far from understanding the essential details of developmental biology, including the exact role of the placenta. It is obvious, too, that any premature application of *in vitro* techniques could cause many more defects than it might prevent. Investigators have already been doing research, mostly with animals, for some time on *in vitro* fertilization; on the freezing and storage of sperm and eggs; on the pre-implantation embryo; on "artificial placentas"; on the transfer of eggs and embryos from one womb to another (especially in cattle) ; on chambers that might keep premature fetuses alive for longer periods of time; on nearly all the aspects of reproductive biology that bear on *in vitro* technology—though this work has lately come under renewed ethical scrutiny.

More than ten years ago, when I was interviewing scientists for my book *The Second Genesis,* a researcher in Michigan told me that he would, if he could, carry an *in vitro* fetus all the way to term. Much more recently— on the same day, in fact, that the news of the first test-tube baby was announced in London—I happened to be having lunch with Dr. Emanuel M. Greenberg, a specialist in obstetrics and gynecology with staff affiliations at two major New York hospitals. When the conversation turned to *in vitro* babies, he took out of his briefcase and handed me his already-expired patent (No. 2, 723,660, dated November 15, 1955) for an artificial uterus. With updated technology and a renewed interest in test-tube babies, Greenberg plans to seek support for the reactivation of his project. And Greenberg is certainly not alone. In *Brave New World,* published in 1932, Huxley was projecting ahead *600 years* to the full development of *in vitro* biotechnics.

Meanwhile, in the course of the preliminary investigations with animals, we will be acquiring enormous quantities of valuable information about developmental biology that is bound to be of great practical use to human beings, whether or not we ever decide to go the *in vitro* route. Meanwhile, too, there is a good reason for going this route with primates. There *is* a growing shortage of primates available for research. Countries in Asia, Africa, and South America that formerly shipped out squirrel monkeys, rhesus macaques, marmosets, baboons, chimpanzees, and other primates in large numbers for biomedical and psychological research have now substantially restricted—even banned, in some instances—further exports of these animals; a few have been placed on the endangered-species list. The cost of primates has, as a result, gone beyond mere inflationary increases; a more efficient means of breeding primates in the laboratory under controlled conditions may turn out to be a virtual necessity for those who want to continue doing primate research. These same considerations could also provide a practical motive for pursuing research in cloning. If these biotechnologies work for primates, moreover, they may also provide partial solutions for other endangered species.

I have not begun to answer the questions I have raised here. I have not even raised the further questions implied by these questions. And I have omitted more than I included. My intention has been simply to explore the issues and to underline my conviction that these issues are worth our concentrated attention. And I am not, as I must seem to be, trying to evangelize on behalf of *in vitro* procreation for humans; I "make the case" for it mainly to demonstrate that there *is* a valid case to be made.

Family and Religious Concerns

Many people (myself included) have expressed concern about the effect these budding biotechnologies may have on human relationships, sexual practices, family stability, and child-rearing. Sex as recreation has long since been effectively divorced from sex as procreation. Now it appears that procreation can be effectively divorced from sex. Presumably there would be nothing compulsory about making use of *in vitro* techniques, no matter how near-perfect or how available they might eventually become; and most people would probably still choose to procreate in the traditional manner. There are, of course, strong religious inhibitions and prohibitions in regard to "tampering with nature" in the ways described. Moreover, such distinguished bioethicists as Paul Ramsey, of Princeton University, and Leon Kass, of the University of Chicago, have issued grave warnings of the threat to the very essence of our humanity and to our civilized self-perceptions if we pursue these procreative technologies. Other bioethicists—among them theologian Joseph Fletcher, of the University of Virginia School of Medicine, author of *Situation Ethics,* and theologian-embryologist Robert Francoeur, of Fairleigh Dickinson University—are more optimistic about our ability to cope with the dangers.

Should Research Go On?

Some ethicists—and some scientists as well—feel such alarm at the prospects as to urge that even the incipient research directed toward these ends *not* be pursued. They believe the potential for ultimate mischief inherent in the manipulation of the procreative process is so great that we're better off without the knowledge. Even to think seriously about pursuing these lines of inquiry, they argue, is to offer evidence that the erosion of our humanity has already begun to take place. Should we then avoid pursuing the search for useful insight and understanding of the developmental process out of a conviction that we're certain to misuse whatever we discover? Such a negative decision would be a confession that we profoundly mistrust our capacity to use our human resources humanely—and that kind of fearful conviction, it seems to me, would offer even more distressing evidence of the erosion of our basic humanity.

I would vote, then, to do the research—not on a crash basis, but with reasonable speed—on animals. I would vote, too, for maximum discussion of the ethical, moral, social, philosophical, economic, religious, and political consequences, with as much public participation as can be elicited. Only after such a thorough airing should any decision be made to make the resulting techniques available to human clients; and then only with adequate safeguards, and with appropriate assurances of efficacy and safety from the responsible scientific community.

All these *caveats* duly entered, it seems to me neither bizarre nor "dehumanizing" to envision a day—though I wouldn't predict how soon it might come to pass—when *in vitro* procreation will have become simply an unconventional, though not uncommon, alternative route to parenthood.

THINKING ABOUT TEST-TUBE BABIES [8]

Louise Brown may have been the first human to make the cover of *Time* before she was even born. The remarkable facts of her conception, in a laboratory dish containing her mother's surgically removed egg and her father's sperm, followed by reimplantation in Mrs. Brown's uterus, provoked cries of "Miracle!" as well as worried invocations of Huxley's *Brave New World*. Thinking about "test-tube babies" seems to fall into three categories:

The anathema response: The entire innovation is morally unthinkable. It is a gross, depersonalizing interference in the "natural" reproductive process. It places risks on a yet-to-be-born person which demand a consent that obviously can never be given. It inevitably involves the foreseeable rejection of fertilized ova, or even the calculated abortion of defective fetuses. In sum, it stands in a line of technological horrors, from gas chambers to nuclear weaponry, and it points directly toward the genetic engineering and assembly-line breeding of Huxley's dystopia.

The assimilation response: Neither the end nor the means involved in "test-tube babies" are drastic departures. The goal is an ancient one: for childless couples to have offspring. The means are but an extension of the human

⁸ Editorial entitled "Test-Tube Babies." *Commonweal.* v 105, no 17, p 547-8. S. 1, '78. Reprinted by permission.

interventions we already accept—in fact, celebrate—when nature proves harsh or recalcitrant. The conception and development of new human life is already regulated or assured by contraception, fertility drugs, amniocentesis, artificial life-support systems and dramatic surgery for the prematurely born. Artificial insemination has been employed for decades without any of the drastic consequences sometimes predicted and now conjured up in connection with *in vitro* fertilization and embryo transfer. As for the inevitable failures and abortions, these too have their counterparts in nature: numerous zygotes fail to implant themselves and defective fetuses are often spontaneously rejected. Genetic manipulation, the use of surrogate mothers, or the total extra-corporeal and extra-familial creation of human individuals are dangers that ought to be faced on their own terms, and not forestalled at the expense of those who could benefit now from medical advances.

The apprehension response: The fact that there are precedents for "test-tube" conception is not reassuring. It demonstrates, instead, the power of science and technology to move us willy-nilly into difficulties we have not demonstrated the will or the skill to resolve. Procreation has been loosened just that much more—and rather decisively—from the knot of personal determinants, sexual intimacy, and marital relations in which it has been bound. If artificial insemination allowed the substitution of a donor's sperm for the father's, now *in vitro* fertilization allows the substitution of a donor's egg for the mother's, and reimplantation further allows the substitution of a donor's womb. The possibilities of moral and social mischief are multiplied. The logic of replaceable parts moves reproduction another step toward the morality of manufacture. Though one may hesitate to term the loss of a fertilized egg the size of this dot (.) an abortion, there is little reason to think that the manufacturing principles of quality control can halt there. Mrs. Brown, after all, was required to agree in writing that she would abort any fetus found to be defective, and no one has inquired as to what period of pregnancy or to what

degree of defect such an agreement extended. However the medical-moral theory of consent might be applied at this stage of life, the idea behind that theory is to prevent the person from being treated as an object, as a "product." Which is exactly what the method of create-and-discard-the-failures threatens to do. Finally, the new techniques consume precious medical resources—scarce human skills as well as money. The promise they dangle before most women with blocked fallopian tubes but without wealth is a false one. Meanwhile the priorities of medicine are further distorted, and attention is diverted from the need to find parents by adoption for millions of already living children.

Of these three responses, the first is simply too naive about "nature" or too negative toward human control. It is unrealistic about the risks that all life imposes—without consent. It is too certain about abortion at the very first stages of development, and too ready to cast scientific or technological developments as dangerous steps on a slippery slope.

Where the first response is dogmatic, the second is deluding. To justify today's developments because they are not much different from yesterday's is truly to pile ambiguity upon ambiguity, to construct a morality on sand. The pattern is clear when defenders of *in vitro* fertilization and reimplantation dismiss concerns about the loss of nascent life by pointing out that abortion is widespread anyway. If the new techniques can be assimilated to traditional human desires and medical aims, the assimilation also works in reverse. Thus Donald Chalkley of the National Institutes of Health is quoted as saying, in justification of the failures inherent in the new methods: "When a husband and wife go to the bedroom and experiment, the experiment will fail two-thirds of the time." Well, that is one way of characterizing what husbands and wives are doing, perhaps a thought-provoking way, but in the end hardly satisfactory.

So we are of the apprehension party. Our apprehension is deepened by the way in which this historic step came

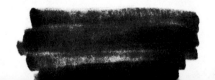

about. Despite long-standing controversy over *in vitro* fertilization and reimplantation, the decision to proceed was entirely in the hands of two interested researchers and a willing couple. There was no groundwork of primate experimentation. Not even the unfortunate trade in publicity surrounding young Louise has revealed many scientific and ethical aspects of the case. *Time* magazine noted "the furious scientific competition between rival fertility researchers," and national rivalry waits in the wings—American researchers have bemoaned the fact that HEW's ethics guidelines kept America from being first with a test-tube baby. All this in the wake of a debate over recombinant DNA that revealed how skin-deep was the scientific community's willingness to entertain any degree of public control. We have discovered how to control the most delicate processes of life but not how to control the processes of discovery.

To be apprehensive is not merely to occupy some middle of the road, worrying aloud while doing nothing. Calls for "public discussion" are not enough. Ethical reservations about *in vitro* fertilization have appeared in medical journals for eight years but talk is cheap when there are still no sanctions against, and many incentives for, scientific *faits accomplis*. The proper step now is to maintain HEW's moratorium on *in vitro* fertilization experiments and to broaden it with legislative and professional restrictions. *Then* let the researchers argue their case. And please, without the cant about Galileo and the Dark Ages. Science is the established church of our era, and every survey shows the public retaining great confidence in its powers. The momentum remains with science and medicine. It is only common sense that the burden of proof should rest on those who would continue with test-tube procreation.

TO FOOL (OR NOT) WITH MOTHER NATURE [9]

"The issue is how far we play God, how far we are going to treat mankind as we would animal husbandry." So says Leo Abse, a British M.P. who has long felt that policy-makers have not dealt seriously enough with the issues raised by developments like the test-tube baby, and plans to lead a parliamentary debate on the matter this week. But for philosophers and theologians, as well as scientists, the Oldham [test-tube baby in England] experiment sharpens some long-standing moral and religious questions. Is *in-vitro* fertilization to be applauded as a humanizing technique, allowing some infertile couples the joy of procreation? Or is it dehumanizing, a step that is to be condemned because it puts the moment of creation outside the body into a mechanical environment?

To some thinkers, the Oldham experiment poses no problems. Says Rabbi Seymour Siegel, professor of ethics at Manhattan's Jewish Theological Seminary: "The Browns were trying to obey the commandment to have children. When nature does not permit conception, it is desirable to try to outwit nature. The Talmud teaches that God desires man's cooperation."

For many others, *in-vitro* fertilization is fraught with moral dangers. British geneticist Robert J. Berry, a consultant to a board set up by the Church of England to consider issues like the ones raised by the Brown baby, accepts the procedure for couples who want a child, but he is still troubled. "We're on a slippery slope," he warns. "Western society is built around the family; once you divorce sex from procreation, what happens to the family?"

For the Roman Catholic Church, which first came out against *in-vitro* fertilization in the 1950s, the Oldham experiment promised yet another round in Rome's long

⁹ Article in *Time.* v 112, no 5, p 69. Jl. 31, '78. Reprinted by permission of TIME, The Weekly Newsmagazine; Copyright Time Inc. 1978.

fight against advances in procreation and birth control. Although the Vatican has yet to take official notice of the test-tube pregnancy, a top official quickly reiterated the church's position that "interference with nature is not acceptable" in any form. For that reason the Papacy has condemned artificial insemination, even with the husband as donor. The church is also opposed to the use of contraceptive devices for the same reason; the Browns' motive is the opposite—to have a child. But that may not matter. Says the Rev. William B. Smith, a spokesman for the Archdiocese of New York: "It's the contraception argument backward. Pius XII talked about not wanting to change the home into a laboratory. I call it switching the marital bed into a chemistry set." Catholics and other Christians who believe that life begins at conception are also troubled by the fact that in test-tube fertilization, many fertilized eggs die.

Some skeptics doubt that enough embryo transplants have been done on primates and other mammals to justify trials on man and also wonder if the patients know enough about the risks to give "informed consent." Protestant Theologian Paul Ramsey insists that the rights of the child-to-be should be considered. He argues that test-tube procreation is "immoral" because of the uncertainties involved: the parents' right to have children is never so absolute as to justify such "induced risk" to the child. Ramsey sees a further risk in Britain's birth watch: possible stigma or damage to the Brown child's self-image because of all the notoriety.

The ethical questions raised by scientific advances in procreation can only become more urgent as new techniques are explored and developed. Robert Edwards, [Patrick] Steptoe's partner in the Oldham experiment, has advocated test-tube selection of the offspring's sex, though only to reduce such sex-linked diseases as hemophilia. Politician Abse fears that "we are moving to a time when an embryo purchaser could select in advance the color of the baby's eyes and its probable IQ."

As for Lesley Brown, she has less difficulty reconciling herself to such anxieties. "I realize that this is a scientific miracle," she told the *Daily Mail*. "But in a way, science has made us turn to God. We are not religious people. But when we discovered that all was working well and I was pregnant, we just had to pray to God to give our thanks. It seemed right and natural."

ARTIFICIAL INSEMINATION: APPLICATIONS AND ETHICAL CONSIDERATIONS [10]

Most couples use AI [artificial insemination] because the husband is subfertile or infertile. But there are many other reasons for using this technique.

One possible use of AID [in which the donor of the sperm is not the husband] is to avoid certain health risks. The main example would be a couple where the husband has a genetic disorder he could transmit to his children. Or he might be Rh-positive while his wife is Rh-negative and has been sensitized against carrying an Rh-positive fetus. In both cases AID with an appropriate donor would minimize the risks to their children.

Frozen semen invites some usual applications because the donor is not restricted by time or location. Fatherhood need not be interrupted by a husband traveling, or living apart from his wife, or even dying. Men killed in war have subsequently fathered children.

Another option is for men to provide ample samples for frozen storage and then have a vasectomy. This was a major reason for sperm banks springing into existence in the 1960s. But even though the price was moderate (today the annual charge is about forty to fifty dollars), sperm banks have not proved as popular as had been expected.

[10] From the book, *Life Manipulation; From Test-tube Babies to Aging,* by David Lygre, biochemist and professor, Central Washington University, Ellensburg. p 9-19. Walker and Company, Copyright © 1979 by David G. Lygre.

One important drawback is that there's no assurance that the frozen samples will later produce children. For one thing, samples from different people vary considerably in how well they freeze; some may be good for ten years or more, while others deteriorate rapidly. Moreover, freezing and thawing generally lower sperm motility, and this decline may be especially severe in samples stored several years or longer. As one physician said, "You pays your money, and you takes your chances."

Another possible problem is that sperm banks aren't tightly regulated, so their quality control could vary. Yet it would be rather important that the semen samples not be mislabeled, misplaced, inadvertently thawed, or accidentally used by someone else.

An unusual use of AI is for women to bear children for unmarried men, or for couples where the wife is infertile. Far-fetched? The following classified ad was placed in a California newspaper: "Childless husband with infertile wife wants test tube baby. English or Northwestern European background. Indicate fee and age." He offered up to ten thousand dollars to anyone who would conceive "his" child by AI and then give him the child after birth. "I'm a very moral man," he said. "I don't want to meet the woman face to face, much less have sexual relations with her."

There have, in fact, been at least three documented cases of women bearing children for the biological father and his wife by AI. And it is likely that there are other, undocumented cases where this has happened. In return for her services, and the baby, one woman received seven thousand dollars and all her maternity expenses.

Unmarried women—both heterosexual and homosexual —could use AID to bear children for themselves. Indeed, this has been done in several countries. These women see AID as a way to become mothers without having to resort to an affair with a man they do not intend to marry.

AI also offers the tantalizing prospect of preselecting the sex of a child. This is because the type of sperm that fertilizes the egg determines the child's sex. While each egg carries an X chromosome, a sperm carries either an X or a Y chromosome. If an X-carrying sperm fertilizes an egg, the child will be female (XX); the Y-bearing sperm will produce a male (XY).

It is possible to control which type of sperm fertilizes an egg? It is becoming clear that the answer is yes. The reason is that the two types of sperm have differences (including size, shape, motility, behavior in an electric field, and sensitivity to acid) that can be used to separate them.

Landrum Shettles, a physician now in Randolph, Vermont, contends sex preselection will work even with intercourse. He has developed procedures to maximize the proportion of the desired sperm type trying to fertilize the egg. The most important factor is timing; intercourse two and a half or more days before ovulation favors girls, while a gap of one day or less favors boys. His recipes also include douches, controlling orgasm in the woman, and the position during intercourse. Shettles has reported that with these techniques, couples have children of the desired sex at least 80 percent of the time.

But his prescriptions are controversial. A few physicians have confirmed that his system works; others are skeptical. One problem is that we need better statistical data for this method, not only on the sex ratios achieved but also on the total pregnancy rate and the health of the children born. Another complication is a report by Rodrigo Guerrero, a physician in Colombia. While he found that AI three or more days before ovulation produced mostly girls and insemination very close to the time of ovulation produced about 60 percent boys, he also reported that the pattern was reversed with natural insemination.

Although sex selection may work with intercourse, it will be far more effective to separate the sperm types and then use AI. For one thing, more complete separations can be made in the laboratory than inside a woman's reproductive tract. And the pregnancy rate could be improved with

AI by combining the treated samples to give high sperm counts before insemination.

It will work. Several separation methods have been tried in animal studies. AI with those samples gives a 60- to 80-percent success rate in producing the desired sex.

Scientists also are learning how to separate the two types of human sperm. For example, the smaller, faster-swimming sperm that bear a Y chromosome are more likely to escape from certain barriers, or to swim over to materials on which they can be collected. One such method produced samples with 85 percent Y-type sperm; another gave 89 to 97 percent Y-type.

The technology is advanced enough that several hospitals are trying this approach with couples who definitely want boys. According to a preliminary report, a medical team at Michael Reese Hospital in Chicago was able to isolate fractions with an average of 67 percent Y-type sperm. Because of a low sperm count, however, the pregnancy rate with those samples is lower than normal. Nevertheless, four of the first six conceptions have been males (67 percent); five of the babies were delivered at term, but one male fetus was spontaneously aborted.

Some Concerns

SAFETY

We might expect that laboratory manipulations would damage sperm and produce abnormal babies. But the data show otherwise. The evidence from animal breeding programs indicates AI is safe and effective. And although we have much less data for human AI, the conclusions are similar. According to one report, a study of twenty thousand children conceived by AI showed an incidence of abnormalities that was no higher than for children conceived by intercourse. There are conflicting reports on whether AI slightly increases the rate of spontaneous abortions, but the few studies with frozen sperm indicate a normal incidence of spontaneous abortions and defective children.

Follow-up studies also indicate AI is safe. When fifty-four AID children were tested for physical and mental development, their only "abnormality" was their above-average IQ scores. The effect on IQ is not surprising, though, for IQ intelligence is one of the criteria used in selecting sperm donors.

But that brings us to a safety problem—screening donors. One physician remarked: "Can I check the validity of their specimen, to make sure they didn't substitute someone else's? No. Can I check their medical history? No. Can I check to see if the person went out the night before delivering the specimen and got VD? No. I've just got to take his word for it." In the real world, a thorough analysis of each donor would be prohibitively expensive, so his stated genetic history is usually accepted at face value. And it is cumbersome, and expensive, to test every sample from every donor for venereal disease. Although there is a two-hour test that detects gonorrhea in most cases, thus enabling the doctor to use the semen fresh, the usual practice is to check a donor's sample occasionally. This means there is some risk. Indeed, there has been at least one instance where gonorrhea was transmitted by AID.

In practice, then, it is necessary to depend on the integrity of the donors and the people screening them. Most donors are interns, medical students, or other graduate students. This arrangement has worked reasonably well, but commercial pressures may develop for more donors. If that happens, the chance to supply semen for cash, trading stamps, or guitar lessons might attract a less lovely crew of donors. A few might even lie about their health if necessary. It would be like the problems with paid blood "donors."

Why would we want more donors? For one thing, there could be a closer match of the donor to the husband. And a wide selection might bring in more customers. Although features could not be guaranteed in the children, the discriminating shopper might be attracted to the catalog: "Donor six and a half feet tall, with high IQ, bulging biceps, music talent, blond hair, violet eyes, and whiter-than-white teeth."

EMOTIONAL EFFECTS

Another concern is that AID (or AIHD) could disrupt family relationships. [In AIHD, semen from the husband and another donor are mixed.] For example, the husband might feel sexually inferior; he may resent the donor and feel separated from his wife and "her" new child. And the wife may feel an attachment to the donor, and the baby growing inside her, but a detachment from her husband.

The problems are real. Consequently, a physician generally will not urge couples to try AID; the impetus must come from them. And before AID is done, there is typically an interview to assess whether both the husband and wife truly want AID and can cope with the psychological problems. Some couples are turned down.

Another safeguard is to select a donor who resembles the husband in race, skin shade, hair color and curl, blood type, and other features. In addition, the donor remains anonymous.

Because of these precautions, alienation is rarely a serious problem. To begin with, couples receiving AID tend to be thoughtful and responsible people with mature marriage relationships. And since AID, in contrast to adoption, lets the couple share the experiences of pregnancy and childbirth, the psychological effects are often positive. In a survey of 102 women who had tried AID (57 had become pregnant), 46 percent believed the experience had strengthened their marriage; the others reported that AID hadn't changed their relationship significantly.

AIHD poses another set of problems, both physical and psychological. When two samples are mixed, the semen from one donor (usually the husband) may impair the other donor's sperm. Another problem is that couples clinging to the slight possibility that the husband would be the biological father may not be mentally prepared for AI involving another donor. So AIHD is rarely practiced. There is another tactic, though, that accomplishes the same thing: A couple could have intercourse the same day as AID.

A difficult issue parents face with AID (and AIHD) is whether to tell their child how he was conceived. The usual advice is that the couple not reveal this to the child, or anyone else. Since the donor is kept anonymous, there is no way for the child to learn who the genetic father is, anyway. But as AID becomes more common, both for married and unmarried women, keeping it a secret may become less popular.

There are few problems with AID children being accepted as part of the family. Indeed, one doctor has written: "These children mean more to families than children conceived in a normal manner. But for artificial insemination, motherhood would be denied the wife. Babies conceived in this manner are wanted children, often desperately wanted. I know of not a single case in my practice where things have worked out badly."

SEX PRESELECTION

One problem with using AI or intercourse for sex preselection is that they won't be 100 percent accurate. So there will be some unpleasant surprises. And when their expectations are not fulfilled, couples may feel more resentment and disappointment than they normally do when they get the "wrong" sex by chance. The child may suffer as a result.

But there is another side to this problem. Even now, without sex preselection, some children are psychologically abused because their parents wanted the other sex. If preselection methods worked most of the time, there would be fewer such children.

Another practical problem with sex preselection by AI is that it will not be cheap. Unless the government or health insurance companies underwrote the cost (ultimately sending us the bill), sex preselection would be an option mostly for the middle- and upper-income families.

Yet there are situations where sex preselection clearly would be beneficial. One use is to avoid having children with diseases such as hemophilia and Duchenne muscular dystrophy, which are carried on the X chromosome. Women who carry such a disorder do not have the disease if their other X chromosome is normal. But their sons will receive their only X chromosome from the egg, so there's a 50-percent chance that they would have the disease. Although half of their daughters (on the average) would be carriers, none would have the disease because they will have at least one normal X chromosome, the one supplied by the sperm. So if the wife were a carrier, the couple could avoid having a child with muscular dystrophy or hemophilia if they could preselect girls. But since no preselection method will be perfect, they would still have to consider a backup plan —diagnosing the sex of their fetus early in pregnancy and aborting in case of a male.

Sex preselection could also affect our population patterns. This prospect has been a great boon to demographers and sociologists, who have yet another topic for their questionnaires and speculations.

One effect would be on family size. Although some couples would decide to have another child if they could be sure of the sex, the larger effect would likely be in the opposite direction: Couples would have fewer children if they could get a child of the desired sex on each try.

Another effect might be an excess of boys. Polls and studies of family reproductive patterns have indicated a preference for having boys, especially as the first child. Amitai Etzioni, a sociologist at Columbia University, has speculated that if sex preselection produced an abundance of males, our society might have less culture, less religious activity, more aggression and crime, increased prostitution, increased homosexuality, and greater interracial and inter-class tensions. It is a fine commentary on the male species.

A survey of six thousand married women, however, indicates the results wouldn't be so drastic. Most parents want boys and girls, with a son coming first. Parents who already have children say they would use preselection mostly to balance the sex ratio of their children. So we could expect an initial surplus of boys, followed by a wave of girls, with a fairly normal sex ratio in the end. And even those mild effects would depend on having a safe, inexpensive, and reliable method available, and large numbers of people choosing to use it. Yet according to the survey, many people would not use it at all.

There is just one snag as far as the sex ratio is concerned. Suppose it turns out for a while, as is the case now, that our methods work better for preselecting boys. . . .

Ethical Issues

AI raises several moral issues that also apply to other techniques we will discuss later. Here we will consider four of them.

INTERVENTION IN NATURE

Some people contend AI is immoral because it is unnatural. For example, the Catholic Church has condemned one feature of AI—masturbation—on these (and other) grounds, or anywhere else.

To begin with, these objections rest on biblical interpretations that are arguable. Furthermore, the issue here is not masturbation in general, but its specific use to supply semen for AI, including AIH [in which the husband's sperm is used]. If this is a serious problem for the couple, however, there is a cumbersome solution: The donor could have intercourse with his partner, and the semen could then be retrieved from a condom, or from her vagina.

Yet even if the semen were collected after intercourse, the recovery of sperm and the insemination itself could be considered unnatural. So here we need to examine a more basic question: Is something that is unnatural therefore immoral?

First, we must decide what we mean by "unnatural." That word generally means anything artificial, anything that violates natural law, or an abnormal pattern of behavior. But it is hard to apply that definition, for we are part of nature. When we develop new ways to manipulate our environment, is this "unnatural"? Is it "unnatural" for us to use our intellect and skills to improve the quality of our lives, both physically and culturally? Hardly.

Then we come to the question of morality. We decided long ago not to endure the consequences of nature where we could intervene to reduce suffering. Indeed, this is the cornerstone of a civilized and humane society. In medicine, for example, we use a wide array of gadgets, surgical methods, and synthetic drugs. If we consider them "unnatural," and if we believe everything unnatural is immoral, we must condemn cesarean sections, bone marrow transplants, heart pacemakers, braces, glasses, kidney dialysis units, hearing aids, tooth fillings, false teeth, artificial hip pins, and many of our anesthetics, antibiotics, and anticancer drugs.

The crucial moral issue is *not* whether certain methods are "natural" or "unnatural"; it is to decide wisely when we should use them. Joseph Fletcher, an ethicist at the University of Virginia, has said: "Socrates thought it better to be an unhappy man than a happy pig. The pig's satisfaction with things as they are contrasts with a human being's struggle to make things better. Willingness to run the risks of requisite change and improvement is what makes human beings human. Humanness is courage married to reason."

The Marriage Relationship

Some people object to all forms of AI (but especially AID) on the basis that God joined procreation with sexual intercourse, and he made them part of the marriage relationship; therefore, other methods of reproduction are immoral because they are outside God's plan. According to Paul Ramsey, an ethicist at Princeton University: "Since artificial insemination by means of semen from a non-husband donor (AID) puts completely asunder what God joined together, this proposed method . . . must be defined as an exercise of illicit dominion over man no less than would be the case if his free will were forced."

Others, who are less certain of the details of God's plan, respond that the essential feature of marriage is the love between the husband and wife; intercourse and reproduction are important manifestations of that love, but they are secondary to the relationship itself. Although an AI child is not conceived by intercourse, and in AID someone besides the husband and wife is involved, the true marriage relationship is not necessarily violated. In fact, experience with AI shows that its major effect, if any, has been to strengthen that relationship. Furthermore, most couples seeking AI are not willfully separating intercourse from procreation; it is not their choice—indeed, it is their misfortune—that they are biologically denied the opportunity to have children by sexual intercourse with each other.

At least AID is far preferable, morally, to an Old Testament practice of adultery. According to *Genesis* 16:2: "Sarai said to Abram: 'The Lord has kept me from bearing children. Have intercourse, then, with my maid; perhaps I shall have sons through her.' Abram heeded Sarai's request."

ADULTERY

Some people contend that in AID the woman is committing adultery with the donor. As we have seen, there is a legal precedent for this view.

Nevertheless, the charge hardly deserves comment. Adultery is commonly defined as "voluntary sexual intercourse between a married person and a partner other than the lawful husband or wife." Yet in AID the donor does not meet the woman; in fact, he does not even know who she is. It is nonsense to equate sexual intercourse with the physical transfer of semen.

Some might argue, however, that in AID the woman is being unfaithful in the psychological sense. First of all, that is not adultery. Besides, this objection is groundless anyway, at least where the husband and wife both give voluntary, informed consent before AID is performed.

There is only one clear link with adultery: A woman could use AID to camouflage real adultery.

OVERPOPULATION

Since overpopulation is a serious concern, we may object to any artificial method, including AI, for producing more people. Yet even though overpopulation is a major problem, it is hard to justify this as a sufficient reason to oppose AI.

First of all, we do not know what the long-term effect of AI will be. Currently, it is a minor factor in our population growth. But as sex preselection becomes an optional feature of AI, the net effect may well be to produce smaller families.

Second, until we require fertile couples to limit their family size, it is simply unfair to insist that, in the name of population control, infertile couples bear no children. On what basis could we justify setting a limit (zero) only for them? Because nature ordained it? If we believed that, we should also oppose the use of hormones and corrective surgery to overcome infertility. We might even accept obstetric problems as fate, and not intervene with fetal transfusions, cesarean sections, and the like. Instead, we could let the baby (and, sometimes, the mother) die in the name of population control, and in the name of bowing to nature.

No, thanks. We ought to intervene where we can to promote human happiness and dignity. The burden of overpopulation rests on all of our shoulders, and infertile couples who could bear children should not be singled out to carry an extra portion of the load. They, like all couples, should consider alternatives such as adoption or becoming foster parents. But they should have the same opportunities, and concomitant responsibilities, as other couples.

III. DEATH WITH DIGNITY

EDITOR'S INTRODUCTION

"It is not a question of dying earlier or later, but of dying well or ill. And dying well means escape from the danger of living ill."

Were it not for the rather archaic flavor of that quotation, a reader reasonably familiar with recent writing in bioethics might assume that it is, in fact, a maxim of one of the figures in that very modern field. Actually, it comes from the writing of an ancient Roman, Seneca. Concern about dying well is not something that has just crossed people's minds. Yet the goal of the good death is no longer the province of philosophers alone; more and more it is being sought by many thoughtful people.

The degree to which Americans, until very recently, seemed to resist any recognition of death, is one of the recurrent themes of a foremost authority on the subject, Elisabeth Kübler-Ross, as the first of the selections that follow points out. But death in America is "no longer a hidden subject." When state legislatures have not recently been wrestling with problems of abortion, they have often been debating "right to die" bills, the pioneer among which became law in California in 1976. These are all aimed at giving the individual the right to die "with dignity," to control his or her own destiny when it becomes obvious that attempts to prolong life actually come down to denying "escape from the danger of living ill."

Generally the control is exercised by giving "informed consent" to withdrawal of "heroic medicine," a term now commonly encountered to describe extraordinary scientific means for keeping people alive, often in the face of a clearly foreseeable end. Such consent is now frequently contained in "living wills," by which a man or woman signifies well

in advance of a grave illness that no such special treatment
is desired if such illness should strike.

The right to refuse treatment is being debated openly
nowadays. The right to be told the whole truth about the
presence of terminal illness is being increasingly demanded,
apparently with positive results. According to a study reported in February 1979 by the *Journal of the American
Medical Association,* 98 percent of 245 physicians polled
reported that it was their policy, in general, to be candid
in dealing with their cancer patients. A study conducted in
1961 had shown that 90 percent preferred not to reveal the
presence of that disease to patients.

Euthanasia is still a taboo word with many, who associate it closely with the Hitler era when the term had
nothing to do with its euphemism "mercy killing." But
passive euthanasia has come into the language as a synonym
for the practice of letting nature take its course in terminal
cases; the attending physician simply refrains from heroic
measures, without, of course, using the term *euthanasia*
itself. Suicide has been perhaps the most unmentionable
subject of all in this field. But many psychologists believe
that recently there has been increasing acceptance of even
that practice when it provides an option for the hopelessly
ill, especially if they are aged.

How truly "informed" can consent be, especially in
cases involving the very young or those adults who have
made no will of the kind described? Some bioethicists
have wondered whether the expression "death with dignity" may not itself be a contradiction in terms, and many
a close relative who has had to stand by and watch a
person die painfully and perceptibly would no doubt share
their doubt. Precisely who decides when a case is actually
hopeless—and has anyone such a right? Isn't the over-
riding goal of medicine to preserve life, and hasn't all
medical research been geared (with increasing success)
toward that end?

And what of the person called on to make the hardest
decisions? The physician may be caught in a real crossfire

—between an oath, a conscience, the perhaps conflicting wishes of the patient and immediate family members, and the law. One of the doctors quoted in the AMA report called "the dramatic change in the malpractice situation" a factor in the new trend toward being candid with cancer patients, since it "encourages physicians to minimize liability by transferring knowledge to the patient."

These questions form the bases of the selections that follow. The first two are a survey of our new approach to death and dying, from *U.S. News & World Report,* and an examination of the new conflicts between law and medicine, from *Editorial Research Reports.* The next articles present reports from hospital experience: an account, from the journal *Science,* of pioneering practice by two hospitals in "helping the dying die" (a rare instance of going public with a program heretofore acknowledged, by other institutions, only off the record) ; two case histories, written for *RN* magazine, from the very personal perspectives of the nurses involved; and the story, from *Science,* of a noted Swiss doctor brought to trial for refusing to maintain heroic measures to prolong the lives of irreversibly comatose patients. This section ends with an article recounting one individual's handling of his dying sister's "living will."

NO LONGER A HIDDEN SUBJECT [1]

Reprinted from "U.S. News & World Report"

Americans by the millions are taking a new and unflinching look at the reality of death and how to cope with it.

From Sunday sermons to best-selling books and televi-

[1] Article entitled "Death in America: No Longer a Hidden Subject," researched and written by Stanley N. Wellborn, associate editor. *U.S. News & World Report.* v 85, no 19, p 67-70. N. 13, '78. Copyright 1978 U.S. News & World Report, Inc.

sion talk shows, people are hearing about a subject that for centuries mainly inspired poetry, religious fervor and, most of all, fear of the pain associated with dying.

Nurturing the death-awareness movement is a growing belief that the individual is losing what many consider a basic right: the power to control one's own dying process.

Added to that are legal and medical controversies over the impact of life-extending technologies on persons diagnosed as incurable. Debate rages among scientists and legislators over the very definition of death.

The dispute erupted last year [1977] in prolonged court battles in New Jersey brought by the parents of Karen Ann Quinlan, a young woman who—her parents felt—was being kept alive by mechanical means although there was no hope of recovery. She remains in a deep coma, but alive, long after her life-supporting devices were shut down.

Such cases point up the new complexity that has overtaken the process of dying.

Before World War I, death in this country was handled by the dying person and the family. Says the Rev. William E. Wendt of the St. Francis Burial and Counseling Society in Washington, D.C.: "Neighbors would dig a grave, and the family doctor would not try to offer hope when none was warranted. Now the dying person is losing control not only to disease but to the medical profession, the funeral industry, the legal system and even the clergy—all saying they know what's best for his last days on earth."

In a recent book, author Jessamyn West described how her incurably ill sister planned and took a lethal overdose of a drug. Euthanasia, West said, may be preferable and more merciful to some than a slow, agonizing and impersonal death.

Dying in Public

Preparation for death, too, is moving out of the realm of privacy into the arena of public affairs.

Major newspapers early this year [1978] published an account of the death from cancer of a young woman, Jane Zorza, written by her parents. Excruciating in detail, the story was profoundly hopeful in overall tone and elicited an overwhelming response from the public.

Senators Hubert Humphrey and Philip Hart emerged as courageous examples to many by continuing to lead active lives despite public knowledge of the debilitating illnesses that eventually killed both.

The new probing of death, its process and meaning, spans all age groups. Academic courses on death are among the most popular new subjects in schools and colleges. Students describe deaths of family members, write their own obituaries, conduct mock funerals and study death in literature and religion.

The widening interest in ways to cope with death has led to efforts in about 200 communities to establish "hospice" care for persons with terminal illnesses. Modeled on institutions in Britain, the hospice provides adequate medical care, companionship and relief from pain for the dying.

For many Americans, however, religion remains the principal bulwark against the fear and pain of death. Even many long lukewarm to religion are intrigued with the so-called life-after-life movement, which claims to have found scientific evidence of a spiritual existence beyond death.

Several recent books that describe the experiences of persons who were pronounced clinically dead, then resuscitated by medical techniques, recall their time on "the other side" as exciting and hopeful. No longer, say these returnees from death, do they fear for their own mortality.

More recently, the traditional funeral and the business practices of some morticians are coming under fire again. A Federal Trade Commission report earlier this year [1978] alleged that certain practices by a number of funeral-home operators annually cost consumers millions more than necessary.

Thanatos: Coming of Age

Scholars see a variety of reasons for Americans' rising consciousness of death at a time, ironically, when humans have conquered most infectious diseases, and longevity in the U.S. is at an all-time high.

Many note simply that in today's wide-open society, death may be the last taboo to be exposed and examined closely. Others point to the estimated 1.9 million deaths in the U.S. this year, 80 percent of which will occur among persons above the age of 65. "These changes have reinforced the idea among many persons that death is something that happens to someone else," asserts Dr. Robert N. Butler, director of the National Institute on Aging. "It has made it easier to examine the subject without feeling that frightening sense of ultimate loss."

Researchers in the growing field of thanatology—from *thanatos,* Greek word for "death"—speculate that the generation that reached maturity during and after the Cold War looks on death with more abstraction. "Young people who grew up with the threat of 'The Bomb' wreaking megadeaths across the globe and who saw life cheapened in the Vietnam experience may be able to view death with more equanimity than previous generations," says Robert Fulton, sociology professor at the University of Minnesota. "There may be a subconscious sense of futility about the future in their minds." Fulton says Americans have long been fascinated by death as an event, citing the continuing investigation of the assassinations of John F. Kennedy and Martin Luther King, Jr., as an example, and prolonged media coverage of plane crashes, murders and suicides.

Other critics say that rock groups called "The Grateful Dead" and films depicting death in artful slow motion seem to show a casual regard for man's fate.

For many, the prospect of life's end is a continuing concern, amounting sometimes to obsession. In his recent movie "Annie Hall," comedian Woody Allen observes: "I'm obsessed with death; it's a big subject with me. I have a very pessimistic view of life."

Few Americans would be so blunt, and many try to disregard the subject. Still, a number of sociologists believe that Allen's remark mirrors the inner thinking of nearly all persons trying to come to terms with their own mortality.

"The subconscious fear of death is the one constant in everyone's life, regardless of their station," says Thomas T. Frantz of the Life and Death Transitions Center at the State University of New York at Buffalo. "Whether we realize it or not, death influences just about every decision we make and every action we take."

The Unmentionable Foe

The modern pioneer in the movement to bring death out of the nation's closet is Dr. Elisabeth Kübler-Ross, whose books describe the stages of the dying process and examine the special psychological needs of dying persons.

Among her most frequently mentioned observations is the way in which humans, and Americans in particular, refuse to admit the fact of death. Among the characteristics of this "death-denying culture," she lists these:

— Americans emphasize youth, beauty and physical fitness. Fewer than 25 percent have wills, and many seem to consider death an embarrassment that should not be discussed openly.

— This country is a leader in the use of heroic medical efforts to preserve life, and commonly isolates terminal patients in institutions throughout their illnesses.

— The denial of death is seen in refusal to give the incurable more control over his or her own dying process and in the stigma against a formal observance of bereavement by family and friends.

Death-denying attitudes, Kübler-Ross believes, should be countered with special therapies that encourage the dying to share their needs and fears. This approach, she feels, enables persons to deal realistically with death in today's mobile, fragmented and sectarian society.

Virtually all modern methods of coping with death are grounded in religious teaching, which sought to establish a relationship between man's life on earth and existence after death. A familiar refrain in much of this teaching is a concept known as "the good death," a public ritual in which a dying person was comforted by family and friends, forgave grievances and prepared for the hereafter.

Today, the good death is seldom experienced. In America, some 70 percent of those who die spend part of their final year in a hospital or nursing home, dying slowly of chronic health problems, often alone. And because of "aggressive" medical care, death often is not allowed to occur quickly and naturally.

Robert M. Veatch, author of *Death, Dying and the Biological Revolution,* comments:

Death, as never before, is looked upon as an evil, and we are mobilizing technology in an all-out war against it. If not death itself, at least certain types of death are beginning to be seen as conquerable. We are being forced to ask the question, "Is death moral in a technological age?"

All this has given impetus to a nationwide effort by many groups to orient society toward a more pragmatic view of the dying process. The movement includes a broad range of alternatives to protect the terminally ill from a fate that many consider worse than death—ostracism and neglect.

At more than 1,000 educational institutions, from elementary grades to medical schools, the subject of death is being discussed openly in formal classes. "Most classroom discussions focus on living rather than dying, and that is one of the greatest benefits of death education," says Daniel Leviton, a professor at the University of Maryland and past president of the national Forum for Death Education and Counseling. "It stimulates us to develop priorities and to communicate our esteem, respect and love to those dear to us before they die."

Other authorities are not convinced. A few school boards have banned the subject because it could lead students into such prickly subjects as religion, euthanasia and abortion. One critic called death-awareness "the new pornography," because of the emotions it arouses.

A bigger concern to Washington's Father Wendt is that death may be "romanticized" in the classroom to the point that the study of death becomes another death-denying mechanism. His view: "This notion of 'death with dignity' that is being taught is preposterous. There is nothing dignified about death."

Helping the Dying—and Bereaved

A remark of the dying, frequently heard by physicians and counselors, is: "I am not so much afraid of death as I am of dying." Surveys show that Americans particularly fear a painful, lonely, debilitating illness. For many, the often-tormenting pain of cancer is the paramount concern.

Arising, as a result, are moral dilemmas that plague the nation's physicians, lawyers and legislators:

Should persons who are clearly moribund be allowed to order an end to the use of life-supporting machines? Should laws specify a definition of death? Is euthanasia proper?

Pleas are heard for the legalization of illicit drugs such as heroin that are shown to be highly effective pain relievers. Stewart Alsop, a political columnist who died in 1974 of leukemia, wrote in the book *Stay of Execution* of his dying and urged that cancer victims be afforded "the illusion of painless pleasure"—the use of heroin. Others have criticized a society in which heroin was obtainable by criminals but was unavailable to citizens dying agonizing deaths. An interagency federal task force has been established by the White House to research the proposal and to investigate other possible methods of alleviating pain. Meantime, nearly 40 nations now permit medicinal use of heroin.

Another proposal is right-to-die legislation that legalizes "living wills," documents that give physicians the patient's informed consent in advance to end medical care rather than sustain life by artificial means. In 1976, California became the first state to approve the Natural Death Act, but it has been interpreted so narrowly that few Californians have made use of it.

Just as thorny is the problem of defining when death occurs, especially when persons are declared dead and their bodily parts are sought for medical transplants. The solution advocated by many as a model is the Uniform Brain Death Act, already enacted by Tennessee and Montana. This law states, "A human body with irreversible cessation of total brain function, as determined according to usual and customary standards of medical practice, is dead for all legal purposes."

"Mercy Killing"

Perhaps most controversial of all is the issue of euthanasia, or "mercy killing." Surveys show that a majority of Americans believe that a doctor should be allowed by law to end an incurable person's life by some painless means if the patient and family request it. Among persons aged 18 to 34, three fifths believe euthanasia is a legitimate option for a dying person.

On the other hand, most religious and legal authorities maintain their traditional opposition to euthanasia. The medical profession has also tended to oppose active forms of mercy killing, but Dr. Ronald J. Glasser, writing in *Family Health* magazine, observes that a useful right-to-die law would be welcomed by many health professionals frustrated by current standards.

He makes this observation: "Doctors have always practiced passive euthanasia [withdrawal of treatment from the dying] . . . but now technology and bureaucracy have gotten in the way of plain common sense.

"It's a burden on us all—on doctors, on state legislatures, and on the patients."

The process of death means fear and suffering not only for the dying but for the family—and most thanatologists believe that the mourning ritual is therapeutic for survivors.

Such traditions as the Jewish shiva and the Irish wake

allow the bereaved to accept the loss and renew their outlook through family and friends. One study found that survivors who viewed the deceased body in an open casket and went through a formal rite of mourning had fewer post-mortem adjustment problems than those who chose a closed casket and a quick burial.

Dr. Butler of the National Institute on Aging says that the bereaved today are often expected to "carry on as if nothing had happened" and the result is often stressful for survivors. "It is quite true that people can die of a broken heart, and the chances are increased when bereaved persons are not allowed to vent their grief," he asserts.

For better or worse, America now seems on its way to becoming a more death-accepting culture. Many scholars believe that the ways in which society cares for its dying, mourns its dead and instills hope in its bereaved is a measure of its regard for human life. As Stewart Alsop reasoned in his own death saga, "Death is, after all, the only universal experience except birth, and although a sensible person hopes to put it off as long as possible, it is, even in anticipation, an interesting experience."

THE RIGHT TO DIE:
DILEMMAS IN LAW AND MEDICINE [2]

The right-to-die movement presents questions which still defy resolution and in some cases its successes have created new dilemmas, especially for the medical profession. For one thing there remains the question of whether an irreversibly comatose patient is actually alive even though the person's breathing and heartbeat are sustained

[2] From pamphlet entitled "Right to Death," by Helen B. Shaffer, contributor. *Editorial Research Reports.* v 1, no 4, p 76-9. Ja. 27, '78. Reprinted by permission.

artificially. Another difficulty is how to establish criteria for deciding when further treatment is useless.

Terminology in legislation is often ambiguous. Incurable illness may apply to persons who still have the prospect of many months or years of a reasonably active life. How can the doctor be sure that the patient's refusal of treatment is not the result of temporary depression caused by the shock of learning that the illness is incurable? Still another question is how much should the patient be told. The view put forth by most supporters of the right to die is that patients have a right to be told exactly what their illness is and the probable outlook with or without treatment. But many doctors insist that some patients do not want to be told everything and that their will to live may be damaged by learning the gravity of their illness.

Adding to the dilemma is the fact that individuals differ in physical and mental reactions to disease and to medication. Disease itself can be erratic, sometimes moving ahead slowly, sometimes racing explosively through the body, sometimes going mysteriously into remission for considerable lengths of time. Decisions in these cases are particularly difficult when the patient is unable to speak for himself.

Concern that breath-sustaining treatment may be applied to a person who is actually dead rather than merely comatose has helped spur pressure for new definitions of death. From as far back as history records, the standard criterion, rarely questioned, was that death ensued when the heart stopped beating and breathing ceased. Since these functions can now be artificially sustained when the patient has apparently lost forever all sensitivity to surroundings or awareness of life, the drive has been to substitute or add "brain death" as a criterion for total demise of the individual.

To date 18 states have enacted a statutory definition of death. Passage of these laws followed the publication in 1968 of new criteria for a definition of death drawn up by the Ad Hoc Committee of the Harvard Medical School.

Among the Harvard criteria are: "irreversible coma"; "no spontaneous muscle movement . . . [or] spontaneous respiration or response to stimuli such as pain, touch, sound or light"; removal from a respirator for three minutes resulting in "no spontaneous breathing"; absence of reflexes indicating no activity in the central nervous system; and a "flat" encephalogram showing no sign of brain wave activity.

Varied Legislation for Redefining Death

The laws, however, are not replicas of the Harvard document. "All 18 states recognize that death may be pronounced on the basis of irreversible cessation of brain function," states a review of brain death legislation published in the *Journal of the American Medical Association* [O. 17, '77]. But the authors of the article say none of the laws "describes in detail the specific criteria for determining brain death." The authors found three major types of laws, all presenting certain problems. One type establishes alternative definitions of death: this is considered a "major flaw" because it seems to indicate that there are two separate kinds of death and could raise suspicion that one type of death might be chosen to facilitate the removal of an organ for transplant by declaring a potential donor dead at an earlier stage in the dying process than a nondonor. This is a touchy problem and one which has caused indignant relatives to sue doctors, charging them with removing the organs prematurely.

A second type of law provides that death ensues if the physician finds respiration and circulatory function have ceased; but if these functions are being supported by artificial means, the doctor may pronounce the patient dead because of an irreversible cessation of brain function. One state, Louisiana, requires that brain death determinations must be made by two physicians and, if organ transplant is contemplated, one of the physicians must not be associated with the transplantation.

Still a third type of law follows the recommendation of

the Law and Medicine Committee of the American Bar Association which was approved by the ABA House of Delegates in 1975. It states simply: "For all legal purposes, a human body with irreversible cessation of total brain function, according to usual and customary standards of medical practice, shall be considered dead." No criteria are offered, leaving that to the doctor or, if necessary, the courts on the basis of medical evidence. A major reason for the variations and complexities of death-defining laws, according to this review, is "the present climate of public mistrust of the medical profession" which "has prompted legislators to enact more complicated laws in an attempt to protect patients from erroneous . . . declarations of death."

Question of the Right to Refuse Treatment

In general, competent adults have the legal right to refuse medical treatment. There are exceptions, however. Robert M. Veatch, in his book *Death, Dying and the Biological Revolution,* cites, for example, a case in which Judge J. Skelly Wright of the U.S. Court of Appeals for the District of Columbia ordered blood transfusions for a woman who had refused them. The judge said that he so ruled because, among other reasons, she had a seven-month-old child and thus "a responsibility to the community to care for her infant." Veatch said he found possibly 100 cases in American legal history involving refusal of medical treatment. "Some of the cases and the rulings . . . have been so complex that legal scholars have stated . . . that the right to refuse treatment is in doubt," he wrote.

The problem arises chiefly in cases of minors and adults who are incompetent to make their wishes known. In a number of cases, judges have overruled religious objections of parents to having life-saving procedures performed on an afflicted child. In other cases, patients with religious scruples have refused to sign documents giving doctors permission to take life-saving measures but indicated they would submit to a court order. Thus they could have their lives saved, according to their wish, without offense to their religious scruples. There have been other cases in which an adult has refused treatment but a relative has sought to overrule the patient's expressed wish by seeking a legal declaration that the patient has become incompetent to make that decision.

Those with foresight who care about their right to die without futile intervention may write instructions that if they should become incompetent measures should not be taken to prolong their lives needlessly. The most popular form which this request takes is the "Living Will" first devised in 1967 by the Euthanasia Educational Council. . . . [See the following selection and the final article in this section.]

One of the consequences of the new concern for the right to die is the impact on the medical profession. Traditionally the doctor has been king in determining what to do for the seriously and terminally ill. Throughout training and practice, the emphasis has been on his duty to save lives rather than to terminate them. Accustomed because of his expertise to relative autonomy in the sickroom, many doctors and their organizations do not welcome intervention of the law into an area which they feel should be governed by medical judgments.

Right-to-die sponsors have brought pressure on the medical profession to take what they consider a more humane as well as a technically expert approach to patient care. They stress treatment of the dying patient in terms of giving comfort, both psychological and physical, rather than merely providing life-extension treatment. The Euthanasia Educational Council, among others, has promoted the development of courses in medical and nursing schools as well as in-service workshops to help doctors, nurses and other hospital attendants overcome their reticence in dealing with the dying in a personal way.

Dr. Christopher Lasch, a University of Rochester historian, believes that doctors are undergoing a change of heart. "There is talk [among doctors] of 'natural' death—letting the patient die at his own speed, without intervention of machines," he writes. "Some hospitals have instituted seminars on 'the dynamics of death and dying' designed to make doctors as well as patients face death without flinching." He considers these "signs of a new humility, in what has become the most arrogant of professions" and possibly "the beginning of an important change in the [medical and scientific] professions in general."

Although withdrawal of "heroic" measures when the outcome is hopeless has received at least some approval by all major church groups, some opposition to right-to-die activity emanates from those who fear legalizing withdrawal may be a first step toward approval of active euthanasia. This view is sometimes presented by "right to life" movement leaders, whose main activities are opposition to permissive abortion.

While there appears to be no disposition in any professional group to press at this time for legalizing active euthanasia, the issue is not entirely dead. *Psychology Today* magazine, for example, . . . printed an excerpt from a book, *Common Sense Suicide,* . . . published in April [1978], which vigorously argues for the right of elderly persons to choose suicide rather than the pain of living "in the near imprisonment of nursing homes or hospitals." Doris Portwood, the author, writes that the subject at least should be reopened to "rational discussion."

HELPING THE DYING DIE [3]

One day a couple of years ago, Mitchell Rabkin, director of Harvard's Beth Israel Hospital in Boston, was walking down a corridor when he came upon a nurse standing outside a patient's room, crying. The patient, upon whom the nurse apparently had lavished particular care, was a man dying of metastatic cancer. A few minutes before, he

[3] Article entitled "Helping the Dying Die: Two Harvard Hospitals Go Public With Policies," by Barbara J. Culliton, news editor. *Science.* v 198, no 4258, p 1105-6. S. 17, '76. Copyright 1976 by the American Association for the Advancement of Science.

had suffered a cardiac arrest and, as the nurse stood help-lessly in the hallway, a crack resuscitation team was bring-ing him back to life. "Why," she asked Rabkin, "can't they let him die in peace?"

Rabkin did not know how to answer her question, but the incident stuck with him and he thought about it a lot. It became, he recently told *Science,* an important factor in his decision to formulate an official hospital policy defining those circumstances in which it would be acceptable, in-deed, desirable, to issue "orders not to resuscitate" a dying patient.

With the help of lawyers, ethicists, and other scholars, Rabkin spent much of last year [1975] drafting a policy which he published in the 12 August issue of the *New England Journal of Medicine* in hope of finding out what people think about it. The same issue also carries a report from the Massachusetts General Hospital (MGH) where a formal policy about letting people die has been in effect for about 6 months. A third article talks about living wills.

It is well known in medical circles that physicians some-times quietly let a patient die. When it seems certain that nothing more can be done, the physician may decide to turn off a respirator or withhold antibiotics or otherwise give up the use of so-called "heroic" measures to keep someone alive when death is imminent. Physicians do it, but they don't talk about it much.

Given the closeness with which this subject has been held, it is noteworthy that the administrators of two major hospitals have decided—independently of each other—to go public. In an editorial in the *New England Journal,* Charles Fried of the Harvard Law School calls their will-ingness to "come out of the closet" an event of the "first importance." Several other lawyers and ethicists contacted by *Science* said they had not yet read or had time to assess the merits of the two hospitals' somewhat different policies but agreed that by opening public debate they are doing something that should have been done long ago.

But the debate can be a thorny one because once the

subject comes up, it leads sooner or later to the emotionally charged question of euthanasia. Physicians clearly do not want what they consider the humane act of letting the dying die to be confused with mercy-killing. So far, no anti-euthanasia group has stormed the doors of either the MGH or the Beth Israel but there is reason to think, because of their stated opposition to living wills, that such groups will see any policy such as these as one step on the path to hell.

It is interesting that the two hospitals that are first to speak out are in Boston, a largely Roman Catholic city where questions of physicians' respect for the sanctity of life were raised so dramatically, and threateningly, in the abortion issue and the trial of Kenneth Edelin (*Science,* 7 March 1974). But on this matter of letting people die, the hospitals may find themselves on safer ground. The Church does not condone euthanasia, but the Pope has said that it is morally justifiable to withhold heroic measures from those who are about to die.

The policies of the two Boston hospitals should be seen, perhaps, only as an initial attempt to come to grips with a difficult fact of life. Neither, really, is perfect. Fried calls them "incomplete and troublesome in various ways."

The MGH policy, called "Optimum Care for Hopelessly Ill Patients," is the work of the hospital's Critical Care Committee headed by Henning Pontoppidan, an anesthesiologist. As is typical of hospital committees these days, in addition to physicians the group includes nurses, a psychiatrist who is also a Jesuit priest, a lawyer, and a patient—in this case, a woman who has recovered from cancer.

Under the new MGH protocol, the first step in the process of determining care for the critically ill is to classify such patients according to the probability of their survival, as follows:

Class A: "Maximal therapeutic effort without reservation."

Class B: Same as A but "with daily evaluation because probability of survival is questionable."

Class C: "Selective limitation of therapeutic measures." In these cases, there might be orders not to resuscitate, a decision not to give antibiotics to cure pneumonia, and so on.

Class D: "All therapy can be discontinued." Class D is generally only for patients with brain death or who have no chance of regaining "cognitive and sapient life"—a Karen Quinlan.

The MGH guidelines, apparently written with the presumption that patients ill enough to be candidates for treatment withdrawal are likely to be comatose, as often is the case, deal in detail with the relationships that should exist among the patient's primary physician, nurses, and other staff, and a new, permanent hospital committee on the optimum treatment of the hopelessly ill. In theory, the primary or "responsible physician" has full authority over the patient's treatment, including the option of rejecting the advice of the committee, or not seeking it at all. But that absolute authority would seem to be somewhat mitigated by provisions in the guidelines such as one that says if the physician does not want to discuss treatment rationale, the director of intensive care can go to the chief of service and the committee can be called into action whether the physician wants to hear from it or not. It would take a courageous, or foolhardy, physician to act against the institutional judgment of his peers, whether it was he who wanted to terminate treatment and they who wanted to keep trying, or the other way around.

The MGH reports that in its pilot study of its guidelines, 209 patients have been classified A to D, but the hospital refuses to disclose how many individuals were assigned to each of those classes, how many were switched from one to another as their health improved or declined, or what the outcomes were. . . . On 15 occasions the committee was called upon to help resolve issues about the appropriateness of classification or treatment.

The main criticism of the MGH policy is that, by focusing on the relationship between the physician and hospital staff, it appears to have little regard for the rights of the patient and his family. Although it does say that no "definite act of commission," such as pulling the plug on a respirator, can be done without the concurrence of the family, the tone of the MGH statement reflects what one ethicist called the "missing patient syndrome."

By contrast, the Beth Israel policy focuses directly on the right of the patient to make decisions about his own care, and is consistent with that hospital's leadership in the patients' rights movement. (In 1972, Beth Israel was the first hospital to draw up a "patients' bill of rights" which is given to every patient at the time of admission.) Although the Beth Israel statement, "Orders Not To Resuscitate," calls for the establishment of a committee, its role seems limited to advising the primary physician on whether the patient's death is so "certain" and so "imminent" that resuscitation would serve no purpose. Once such a decision is made, on what Rabkin defines as "physiologic grounds," responsibility for actually deciding to issue orders not to resuscitate shifts to the patient and his family, which can give consent for a patient who is not able to speak for himself. Where there is no consent, there can be no orders not to resuscitate.

Whereas the Beth Israel position outdoes that of the MGH in its expressed concern for patients' rights, it falls short with respect to medical scope, dealing only with cardiac resuscitation rather than the full range of death-prolonging technologies. Rabkin says he hopes to remedy that this year.

One potential solution to the dilemma over the patient's right to give informed consent at a time when he may be unable to do so is the so-called "living will," in which an individual declares his desire not to be kept alive at all costs. In the third article of the *New England Journal's* trilogy on the right to die, ethicist Sissela Bok calls the best known of the living wills, that of the Euthanasia Education Council (*Science*, 26 December 1975), "vague in such a way that real risks of misinterpretation arise"—it refers to but does not define "physical and mental disability," for example. She proposes a version of her own.

Unlike other versions of a living will, Bok's will is written as an order, not a plea that others will be good enough to see things your way, and it provides space to authorize two persons—relatives, friends, lawyers, whomever—to see to it that one's wishes are carried out. In addition, the Bok will leaves room for the inclusion of very personal instructions. She has in mind the fact that some patients might want pain-killers, even in amounts that might hasten death, while others would not. One person might want to be kept informed of his condition, no matter how bad, while someone else would not want to know.

Bok's version of a living will has the advantage of meeting many more contingencies than do others. But it also requires more thought and effort on the part of anyone wishing to execute it which, one could argue, is the way it should be. (At present, no state recognizes any version of a living will as legally valid. . . .)

One of the great unresolved issues in this whole matter of helping the dying to die is the legality of withdrawing or withholding treatment. Fried reports there has been little litigation on the subject and not much in the way of legislative law. As long as a patient is mentally competent, there is no doubt about his legal right to refuse treatment. In fact, to force treatment on such an individual could be considered battery. It is when a case can be made that the patient's judgment is impaired that problems arise. As Fried explains it, once a physician begins to treat a patient, he assumes an obligation to do everything that is reasonable on his behalf. To do otherwise would be negligent. The hard question then becomes, What is "reasonable"? And that is something about which there is not much agreement.

Decisions, Fried predicts, are going to end up being

made by juries as cases are brought before the courts, and that is where legally binding living wills and formal hospital policies may come to have their greatest effect.

With respect to hospital policies on withdrawing or withholding life support, Fried believes they could be important in helping a jury assess the "reasonableness" of a physician's action—it could be argued that it is reasonable to act in accord with hospital policy. However, he doubts that any policy, of itself, could ever provide immunity from prosecution.

There are problems with the prospect of hospitals establishing formal guidelines for the care of those about to die, and the greatest may lie in the inevitable fact that committees will now be introduced to a facet of human life that many people believe is already too much in the hands of institutions. As a surgeon from Walter Reed Army Hospital said in a letter to Fried, official guidelines will benefit only lawyers and administrators, while making it infinitely more difficult for physicians to do for the dying what most of them have been doing all along.

On the other hand, the idea has its virtues, one of which is that guidelines would let physicians, hospital personnel, and patients and families know where they stand. It is fanciful but not inconceivable to imagine a time when patients might choose one hospital or another on the basis of its particular policy, assuming that hospitals in any community have clearly different views about the right thing to do.

"The idea that we will ever reach a consensus on these matters is ridiculous," says Fried. "What I'd like to see is the evolution of a more flexible attitude, an admission that wishing to die is not always unreasonable." What we need is room enough to allow for individual choice.

NURSES AND THE RIGHT TO DIE:
TWO CASE HISTORIES [4]

Case I

When did I realize that Mrs. Keidel would present more of a challenge than I'd ever expected?

She was admitted to our med/surg unit one afternoon because of rectal bleeding. "Not too difficult to manage," I told myself, weighing the impact of this new patient on our already busy floor. I glanced at the rather sketchy details on her chart. Vital signs: normal. Age: 84.

I went down the hall to see for myself. Mrs. Keidel was pale, but didn't appear to be in great distress. In fact, she was quite chipper for a person her age. But the most striking thing about her was her friendliness, a warmth that seemed to soften every patient and staff member who came in contact with her.

The change that was to come over her gave me the first clue. Mrs. Keidel made increasingly frequent, sometimes unreasonable demands for attention. We couldn't help liking her in spite of those demands, but as time went on, her behavior seemed more and more out of character. Behind the cheerful, composed surface I'd seen on admission day was a very anxious woman.

She had reason to be. Her bleeding was caused by carcinoma of the intestine. When the doctor told her, I expected tears, denial, anger, and bitterness—but there were none of these. Only anxiety, and endless apologies for demanding so much of our time for the numerous linen changes prompted by the bleeding.

I prepared myself for the battle to save Mrs. Keidel's

4 Article entitled "Are You Too Sure of Your Stand on the Right to Die?" *RN.* 41:74-6+. D. '78. Case I, by Mary Sue Gates, R.N., former staff nurse; Case II, by Gloria Gilbert Mayer, R.N., B.S.N., Ed.D., F.A.A.N., associate chief, nursing service for research, Veterans Administration Hospital, Minneapolis. Reprinted through the courtesy of *RN* Magazine.

life. I expected the doctor to order administration of replacement fluids and to schedule her for bowel resection. But, to my amazement, he didn't.

Because the blood loss was slow, we could build up Mrs. Keidel's blood volume with I.V. [intravenous] and oral fluids, which I encouraged. But her hemoglobin continued to fall at a fairly rapid rate. I asked the doctor if he planned to transfuse her.

"No," he said, "She's ready to die."

I tried to keep cool, but I could feel my blood pressure rising. Just what did he mean by that? Was he trying to play God? Did he think anyone over the age of 70 wasn't worth saving?

The days wore on. Mrs. Keidel continued to bleed, and her color became paler and paler. I'd arrive on my shift, look in on her, and, appalled at her deteriorated condition, have to stifle my impulse to shake her and ask her, "Do you *really* want to die?"

I wanted to persuade her to want to live again—to fight for life with all her strength, right to the last minute.

It went against everything in me, everything I was trained for, to watch her slip slowly into confusion, then into unconsciousness, and finally into death. I was used to seeing everything possible being done to save a life—no matter what the price.

I couldn't bring myself to speak civilly to her doctor. I seethed with resentment. As our entire array of medical techniques and saving devices lay idle, my frustration mounted. Then a peculiar thing happened.

In Mrs. Keidel's last few hours, I began to realize what the price of heroic measures would have been for her. She was full of cancer, and to resect the bowel would have been only a temporary solution. More than anything, I saw, she hated being a burden, dependent on her family. So Mrs. Keidel had calmly decided she had everything to die for. She believed she was going to her Maker, and that she'd be happier than she'd ever been in life.

Who was to stop her?

At last, I understood that I'd wanted to fight for Mrs. Keidel's life mainly because it made *me* feel uncomfortable to watch her die. I wanted her to live so that *I* wouldn't have to face death.

Mrs. Keidel taught me to accept inevitable death in my patients without feeling as if it were somehow my fault that they died.

I still believe in treating the whole patient—I'm still dedicated to saving lives—but not at all costs.

Case II

I was a clinical specialist—an expert with plenty of experience as a hospital nurse, as a faculty member of a prestigious baccalaureate school of nursing, and as a private duty nurse for selected patients. I used to express my feelings on ethical issues with decisiveness. I was *sure* of my views about euthanasia. I was *sure* I could tell black from white, right from wrong. After I met Mr. Barone, I was no longer that sure.

Mr. Barone was suffering from massive gastrointestinal bleeding, cause unknown. At age 78, he was quite alert and oriented, although his condition was deteriorating quickly: hemoglobin, 8 gm/100 ml; hematocrit, 23; vital signs, unstable; pulse, rapid and thready; skin, cold and clammy; conditon—critical.

Resentful of the indignities of illness and treatment, Mr. Barone had decided that his time was up. He wanted control in death as he had known it in life. But his family felt differently.

His daughter, his son, and all their relatives hovered around his hospital room, deeply concerned. Together with his physicians, they decided to do everything in the power of medical science to restore life and health to the old man —regardless of what discomforts that involved.

Rx: Ice lavage q. h. [every hour].

The Barones waited in the family room; watching the process of "freezing" someone who's alert is not pleasant. The doctors came into the room, checked on the progress of the treatment, and left again to study their charts and lab results, and consider their next moves.

I stayed alone with Mr. Barone, to pack him in ice, drench him with ice water, and watch him shiver uncontrollably, hour after hour. My hands obeyed, but my mind rebelled.

Finally, Mr. Barone grabbed me by the collar, pulled me close to his trembling lips, and pleaded, *"Let me die! Stop this indignity!"*

I told his family. And I told his doctors, but they didn't alter their treatment goals.

At the end of that shift, I signed off the case, absolutely certain that the patient's right to die was being violated. I *knew* that prolonging Mr. Barone's life was inhumane. I *knew* we should just keep him comfortable and let him die in dignity and peace. I couldn't understand why I was the *only* one who knew the right thing to do!

I couldn't sleep for several nights, thinking about Mr. Barone. I wondered what happened to him. I wondered how much torture he'd endured before succumbing. I hoped his physicians and family were satisfied, after losing the patient anyway. After four days, I couldn't resist going upstairs to find out what happened.

I couldn't believe what I saw. There sat Mr. Barone, playing checkers with his grandson, alive, looking healthy and in fine spirits. I walked over hesitantly. He looked up and smiled. "Do you know me?" I asked.

He didn't. I asked him if he remembered the evening he was so sick . . . the ice bath? No, he didn't, although his doctors told him he was pretty close to death one night. Mr. Barone had no memory of that terrible evening —and now he was on the mend! A full year later, when I saw him on a routine clinic visit, he was still in fine shape.

I still believe that, in certain instances, people have the right to refuse heroic measures to prolong life—but now I also ask, who is to define those instances? And whose job is it to make the irreversible decision—the doctor? The family? The patient? The nurse?

I'm so thankful no one listened to me that night when I was caring for Mr. Barone. It frightens me to think that if we'd quit trying to save him and he'd died, I'd have felt even more thoroughly convinced that I was right all along. Mr. Barone wouldn't have been around to challenge me. And I wouldn't have given my attitude toward the right to die a second thought.

IS PASSIVE EUTHANASIA MURDER? [5]

Early on the morning of 15 January [1975], Urs Peter Haemmerli was arrested at his home in Zurich, having been accused of murder. Two policemen came knocking at seven o'clock. Haemmerli recalls that they politely waited for him to dress before taking him off to jail. At first he thought it was a bad joke. "After all," he reasons, "if I had murdered someone, I would be the first to know it."

As it turned out, Haemmerli was not accused of murdering "someone." He was accused of murdering by starvation an unspecified number of unnamed elderly patients at Triemli City Hospital, where he is chief of medicine. The alleged murders are said to have taken place during a period of four years. For months, lawyers have been combing the hospital's records in search of a victim. No formal charges can be pressed and the case cannot proceed unless he can be accused of murdering someone in particular. Haemmerli optimistically bets that no murder victim will ever be found and that his case will never come to trial. But the fact that it has come up at all sets a precedent for cases involving passive euthanasia.

As the accused recounts it, this is how the "Haemmerli affair" came about.

In the spring of 1974, a woman named Regula Pesta-

[5] From article entitled "The Haemmerli Affair: Is Passive Euthanasia Murder?" by Barbara J. Culliton, news editor. *Science.* v 190, no 4221, p 1271-5. D. 26, '75. Copyright 1975 by the American Association for the Advancement of Science.

lozzi was elected to the Zurich city council and named as the city's chief health officer, a position that put her in charge of the municipal hospital system. Haemmerli was pleased. During her campaign, Pestalozzi, a layperson, had called for improved care for the elderly and the chronically ill. At Triemli, described as Zurich's newest and most modern municipal hospital, there were many such patients. Haemmerli thought that he would have a friend in court in the new health officer. He invited her to visit Triemli. Months passed but she never came. Then, in December, she asked him to visit her, and one day the doctor and the politician had a long conversation in her office. Haemmerli remembers it as a very pleasant occasion.

Among other topics, Haemmerli and Pestalozzi talked about the care of the terminally ill. Haemmerli does not believe in giving extensive treatment to a patient who is hopelessly ill; sometimes, he believes, it is better to allow a person to die in peace. Take, for example, the case of a person who has a stroke, lapses into a coma, and, after months, has not regained consciousness—who, in the opinion of the medical staff (both doctors and nurses), is never going to be conscious again. That is the example Haemmerli took with health officer Pestalozzi. The patient is unconscious but still breathing. "In the case of such patients, the cerebrum has failed irreversibly, so that they have permanently lost consciousness. However, their deeper brain structures are only partially affected, so spontaneous respiration goes on." These patients are kept alive by artificial feeding, usually through tubes that pour solutions of nutrients directly into their stomachs. Eventually, the question is asked, Should this continue? As far as Haemmerli and his staff are concerned, the answer is no, and feeding is discontinued. In its place, the patient is given only a solution of salt and water that prevents dehydration and maintains the normal balance of chemicals in the blood. Usually the patient dies within a couple of weeks. In fact, it is death by starvation. As far as anyone knows, for a comatose patient it is painless. Haemmerli calls it "sound and humane" medical practice and adds, "I have never done anything to my patients that I would not do for my own mother and father, who are still living, if they were in such a position."

Pestalozzi, Haemmerli recalls, seemed interested in what he had to say but asked no questions about it. He left her office. As far as he knew, "That was that." A month later, the police came. Following the accusation of murder, Haemmerli was suspended from the hospital by the city council and barred from seeing his patients. He spent subsequent weeks secluded at home, reading about euthanasia and law. On 1 April, he was reinstated as chief of medicine and has been at work ever since.

Haemmerli feels he was made the scapegoat for the sake of Pestalozzi's political ambition. "She wanted to run for the national government," he claims. "She saw herself as the first woman in the Swiss cabinet. But she was an unknown. She needed some way to get national attention and I was the way. The whole thing was political, even the police knew that. Under our law, they could have held me in jail. We have no bond as you do. But after 15 hours, I was out. I had an engagement to go boar hunting in France and I asked them if I could go. They said 'Fine.' So I went and took my rifle (Haemmerli comes from an old Swiss family of precision rifle makers) and I thought 'Here I am accused of murder and the police say I can go around with a gun. This is not a case of murder. It is a case of politics.' "

Whatever Pestalozzi's motives were for bringing the case, her action brought her at least fleeting fame in Switzerland and all of Europe as the news of the case hit the papers and news magazines, where it was frequently played as a cover story. She became a contender for national office, and she lost.

Haemmerli, too, was thrust into the spotlight, cast in a role he says he would never have chosen for himself but which he has decided to accept for the "good of the profession."

Haemmerli, who stands about 6'4", is the personification of the learned physician and professor. Conservative in dress, precise in speech, sincere in manner, he seems well cast in his role as chief of medicine at one of Zurich's leading hospitals and as professor at the University of Zurich from which he received his medical degree. A specialist in gastroenterology with a particular interest in liver disorders, Haemmerli spent several years in training in the United States at institutions including Mount Sinai Hospital in New York and the medical schools of Georgetown and George Washington universities in Washington, D.C. In 1956, George Washington named him "outstanding resident of the year." "Dr. Haemmerli's devotion to his patients and his ability in instructing interns and students has been an example for the entire George Washington medical service," the citation said. His reputation as a physician continued to climb.

Now, in a more public arena than the medical circles in which he has lived, his reputation is set as an expert on euthanasia, which he finds disturbing and inappropriate. "I never really thought much about euthanasia before this," he notes,

and I am not an expert on the subject. But I know that whenever anyone has a panel on euthanasia, they will invite me to speak and I sometimes will. If my case can help other physicians who find themselves in my position, I will have done some good. I cannot avoid the role.

Indeed, that is the case. When I met him, he was in New York as a guest of the Euthanasia Education Council, at whose meeting he was to be a star attraction. His speech to that group marked his second public appearance since his arrest. The first took place last April when he addressed the Council of Europe [18 European states dedicated to democratic principles], which is in the process of drafting a resolution on patients' rights, the right to die being prominent among them. The Council has yet to complete its work but has already accepted certain proposi-

tions as important. One is that physicians should respect
the will of the sick. Another holds that the prolongation
of life should not constitute the overriding purpose of
medical practice.

As Haemmerli suggests, the time may have come to
redefine the professional duty of the physician, which
has always been defined primarily in terms of action. "In
medical school and postgraduate training, the doctor is
taught to act, to use the scalpel or drugs or machines to
save the patient and restore health. He is not trained in
omitting to act," he observes. Perhaps now he should be.
"The development of modern medicine confronts the doctor with a new problem of principle: 'To do or not to do,
that is the question.'"

The Quinlan case and the Haemmerli affair point up
a feature of public debate on passive euthanasia that is
difficult to deal with. For months the United States public
has been looking at a photograph of Karen Quinlan as she
used to be—calm, pretty, a typical high school senior. In
Europe, people have been given a similarly distorted view
of reality in photographs accompanying stories about
Haemmerli. There have been pictures of well-coiffed
elderly women smiling from their rocking chairs. Grand-
mother. Frail perhaps, but you wouldn't want to let her
die. The German weekly *Der Spiegel* ran a cover picture
of a young woman lying peacefully in a bed with a huge
syringe lying on her abdomen. Thoughts of mercy killing
come instantly to mind.

But Karen Quinlan, who has been described as having
shriveled into a fetal position, should not be confused with
Sleeping Beauty, and the elderly patients whom the staff
of Triemli hospital let die are not relaxing in rocking
chairs. They are comatose, and have been for months. They
weigh practically nothing. Their skin hangs in heavy folds
on their skeletons. And the only thing that keeps them
alive is force-feeding, a procedure that can be extremely
unpleasant. "These patients must be fed through gastric
tubes pushed down their throats," Haemmerli explains,

"and that can make even comatose patients retch and vomit." These patients are not fed intravenously because of the great risk it poses. Once you introduce an i.v. needle into a vein, you introduce a high risk of infection that could lead to fatal embolisms. The patients, who are virtually immobile, expend hardly any metabolic energy. They can survive on only 300 calories a day. Eventually, those calories are withheld and water and saline are substituted. "I see these poor people suffering and I ask myself whether it is my duty to prolong their misery. I do not think it is. It is my duty to make them as comfortable as possible in their dying days."

Haemmerli pushes hard to make clear the type of patients he is talking about. "These are not people who are just senile. They are not healthy except for a single infirmity that makes them unable to take care of themselves. They are brain-damaged and it is irreversible."

The staff members caring for the patient make a collective decision to withhold nutrients when the time comes. "If even one person feels it is not time, we do not withhold," Haemmerli declares. What about the consent of the family? That is a different matter. Haemmerli says he talks to the family but it is clear he does not have high regard for consent. "Informed consent is something that is really only good for the physician. It is a matter of salesmanship. The physician can persuade the family to consent if he wants to. It is meaningless. Furthermore, in dealing with the family, you must consider whether they will act in the patient's interest or their own. Some people will give consent because they can't wait to inherit the patient's money. Sometimes, it is the other way. There have been families that have said, 'You must keep the patient alive until his brother or whomever dies for the sake of our inheritance.' "

In choosing passive euthanasia, Haemmerli believes that irreversibility of the patient's condition is the most important point. In his address to the Council of Europe, he suggested that irreversible loss of brain function be accepted as the definition of human, as opposed to biological, death. It is, he says, a definition that would extend already existing definitions of brain death. Those definitions, written with organ transplantation in mind, deal with total brain death, which includes destruction of brain functions that control the autonomic nervous system; there is no spontaneous breathing, but the body is kept on a respirator long enough for donor organs to be secured. "Probably more frequent in everyday practice, however, are patients whose brains have died but who have preserved their spontaneous respiration," says Haemmerli. The feeding and drugs that keep these people alive are, in his opinion, just as artificial a means of supporting life as is a respirator.

Acknowledging that irreversibility is difficult to determine, Haemmerli says, "What is important . . . is an adequate period of observation. . . . In the case of heart arrest an observation period of less than an hour is enough. . . . In the case of failure of the brain function with continued spontaneous respiration, weeks and often months are necessary."

Once the determination of irreversible brain loss has been made, Haemmerli sees no distinction between pulling the plug on a respirator and withholding antibiotics or nutrients. In his hospital, he says, it is unlikely there would ever be a Karen Quinlan because they would not get caught up in the semantics of whether pulling the plug is a special sort of "act" just because it is so physical and easy to visualize. Haemmerli would pull the plug because he would think it "pointless" not to, not because he would think of himself as practicing euthanasia.

"Lawyers and other persons alien to medicine often find it hard to grasp this concept of pointlessness," Haemmerli told the Council. "For the doctor there is 'point' in any therapy which seems to him likely to succeed. . . . But if it is unsuccessful and if no other therapeutic possibilities exist, then the treatment begun clearly becomes pointless."

It is apparent that some changes are going to have to

be made in order to come to grips with the terrible dilemma that medical technology has created. It may be true that what is needed is a new definition of the physician's duty, as well as a definition of death that distinguishes between "human" death and "biological" death. There is little doubt that such definitions will be difficult to formulate and initially controversial, particularly to individuals who may see them as undermining the value of life and opening the way to abuse. Nevertheless, they will have to come. As Haemmerli says, "All discussion and any new definitions and conclusions resulting from it should satisfy two simple criteria: common sense and the humanitarian principle." [As reported in a later issue of *Science* (194:588. N. 5, '76), a Swiss court subsequently cleared Dr. Haemmerli of the charges brought against him. The court found: "One cannot accuse a doctor of manslaughter if he decides to withhold nourishment from a patient whose human personality has been lost due to severe brain damage."—Ed.]

THE LIVING WILL [6]

I read the words slowly, holding in my hand a small document called A Living Will that I had just found in my sister's belongings. At the bottom of the will was my sister's signature and the signatures of two witnesses. It was dated about two years ago, a time when my sister had been well and active, a widow in her early 70s, a free and independent woman with lots of friends and lots of strength. Now she was in a hospital, dying, while doctors and nurses strove to keep her alive with intravenous feedings, oxygen, and all the marvels of modern science.

And as I finished reading the living will I wondered what to do. I was in charge of her affairs; I was solely

[6] Article by Harry Bernstein, free-lance writer. New York *Sunday News* Magazine. p 13-14. D. 31, '78. By permission of the author.

responsible for her, and it was up to me to see that this will was carried out. Still, I hesitated. . . .

Perhaps my sister's troubles began long before we became aware. Her confused state became noticeable about a year ago and she had gone into the Long Island Jewish Hospital for a complete neurological workup. The verdict: Alzheimer's Disease, an untreatable affliction of the brain. From the hospital she went directly into a nursing home, and the deterioration came on swiftly. In a few months she had the mentality of a child. Then one night she suffered a stroke and was transferred to a hospital in a coma. A week later there was a heart attack. There was now very little left of her. She was crippled not only mentally but physically—the one thing she had always dreaded.

She had mentioned it often, almost as though she had a premonition of what was going to happen. She had also mentioned the living will several times. I had paid very little attention to it.

Euthanasia is a Greek word meaning "good death," but the organization that publishes and distributes A Living Will, Concern For Dying (formerly the Euthanasia Educational Council) insists that the will is a passive form of euthanasia and does not give anyone permission to end the life of another in a "mercy-killing." It is simply a document, they say, stating that the signer does not want to have his or her life prolonged artificially after the doctor decides there is no hope for recovery. Three million copies of the will have been distributed in the United States. A similar type of will called the Mercy Will is published and distributed by the American Euthanasia Foundation, Inc., and many individuals have prepared their own living wills, for personal reasons or to conform to the requirements of the laws of the state in which they live.

Not everyone agrees with the definition of the living will. Right To Life Committee, Inc. calls it "a contract for death," and Jean Head, R.N., chairman of the New York City chapter, says, "We don't need it. The only purpose it serves is to make things easier for the doctor and the relatives—not the patient." She believes in making every effort to keep the terminal patient alive until death comes naturally. "How can you tell," she asks, "when it is actually the end?" And she cites cases of patients who, seemingly close to death, have made miraculous recoveries.

Mrs. A-J Levinson, executive director of Concern For Dying, in turn stresses the great number of people who have been spared needless suffering and agony through the living will. But most important, she says, "It is the individual, not the doctor or the court, who has a right to say how he should be treated when dying." She adds: "We fully support every means possible to keep a patient alive—if that's what they want, and if they have not left a living will."

Is the living will legally binding? Since it has never been tested in court, no one can say definitely, and there are conflicting opinions. Former Sen. Edward Gurney has said, "Generally, it can be stated that euthanasia, whether voluntary or involuntary, and whether by affirmative act or omission, is a violation of existing criminal law." Law professor Arval A. Monis backs this up: "Today, if a physician motivated solely by mercy, consciously and deliberately kills his suffering patient in a painless manner at the request of the patient, his act is considered to be murder—probably in the first degree."

Despite all this, a Living Will has been included in "Modern Legal Forms," which is widely used by lawyers. Also, eight states have thus far adopted Right-To-Die laws, which include allowing adults to execute legally binding documents similar to the living will. New York, New Jersey and Connecticut are not among those states, but all have similar legislation pending, as do many other states throughout the country.

Can a doctor be sued for malpractice for adhering to a living will? C. Dikerman Williams, an attorney who has had much experience in this field, doesn't think so. In fact, he believes that the opposite might be true: a doctor might be sued with a better chance of success by the patient or his estate for the pain, suffering and expense caused, should he continue treatment despite protest by the family of a patient who signed the will.

Most lawyers, however, feel that such a suit would be unlikely. One of a similar nature was tried recently. It involved a dispute between a New York City Hospital and the wife of a man with an irreversible brain damage over the insertion of a new battery in the pacemaker that was maintaining his cardiac function. The physicians did not see the man's condition as terminal and considered it necessary to continue the treatment. The wife felt that her husband's condition did not justify the use of major surgical procedures. A court held that the physicians were correct and appointed a guardian for the patient.

Religious leaders are equally divided on the subject. The opposition base their objections on the Sixth Commandment: "Thou shalt not kill." It assumes that any act terminating a life from motives of compassion or mercy can—if permitted by law—be inspired as well by evil motives. Supporters of the living will are quick to point out that Pope Pius XII sanctioned the use of pain-killing drugs to terminally ill patients, even though these drugs might shorten the patient's life. Catholics deny, however, that this sanctions passive euthanasia, and claim that the Pope condemned euthanasia in both its passive and active forms.

The pro-living will faction point to other religious groups who have taken a positive stand on the question. The United Methodist Church, for example, asserts flatly the "right to every person to die in dignity without efforts to prolong terminal illness merely because the technology is available to do so." Jewish law forbids euthanasia, but Rabbi Bernard S. Raskas of Temple Aaron, St. Paul, Minn., maintains that according to Jewish law also, when a person suffers irreversible brain damage he is considered a "vegetable," and it thus becomes an act of compassion to spare the family the suffering of artificially prolonging the life of this person.

How do doctors feel about all this? Doctors are committed by oath to preserve life and a great many steadfastly refuse to deviate from that oath. Dr. Laurence V. Foye, director of Education Service, Veterans Administration, is one of these. He believes that a doctor must fight to the end to keep his patient alive, that incurability must not be equated with hopelessness.

On the other hand, Dr. Robert Glasser, a physician who heads the Kaiser Family Foundation, states that what he calls "negative euthanasia"—refraining from the use of circulatory and respiratory devices and withholding fluids and gastric feedings—is a legitimate approach to the care of patients with massive brain damage or advanced terminal illness.

And what about the average American? Where does he stand in the debate? According to one Harris survey, 71% of Americans believe a terminal patient has the right to direct his doctor to cease use of life-sustaining machines when there is no cure in sight. This position has been supported by the AMA policy adopted in December 1973 and subsequently up-held by various lower and higher state courts, notably the Supreme Court of New Jersey.

And what about me? How did I stand on this matter? When I sat there at my desk holding a copy of my sister's signed Living Will in my hand, I felt that it was not for me to make any decision. That decision had been made by my sister already, and only she had the right to do so. But what made me hesitate was a question that Right To Life's Jean Head has asked: "How do you know that the patient who signed this will would not in these last moments, when the ability to express is no longer there, change his or her mind?"

I had to think for a long time, and I had to remember the strength that my sister once had and the durability of her mind before that mind began to crumble. There was also something that my daughter told me. She had been very close to my sister, and one day, in the nursing home, when they were alone together, my sister asked, "I wonder what it would cost to die."

My daughter replied, "It would cost you your life."

My sister thought a moment, then shrugged and said, "That's not much."

She had not changed her mind then nor later when she was lying in bed in the hospital, after her stroke and her heart attack, with an oxygen mask clamped to her face and tubes protruding from her nose and arms, and she looked up at me with that desperate, mute appeal in her eyes. I knew what she was trying to say.

I presented her living will to the hospital. Somehow, I doubted that they would take it seriously as a valid document, but a bit to my surprise they did. They had copies made, and distributed these copies to the doctors involved and placed one in her chart.

Only a week later it happened, another stroke, coma. I do not know everything that happened, because I was not there. But I had been there on the two other previous occasions, and I had seen how they rushed her into the intensive care unit, and how doctors and nurses worked over her for hours until they had brought her around. This time, I am told, she was not moved from her room, and she died quietly and peacefully within the hour.

IV. THE ETHICAL USE OF MEDICAL RESOURCES

EDITOR'S INTRODUCTION

Sometimes death is a matter of expiring not with dignity but out of necessity. The necessity stems from a scarcity of medical resources; it becomes impossible to save everyone who is dependent on the limited supply of a drug or of a particular machine or organs for transplantation. The matter then comes down to a round of decision-making that can be summed up by the questions, Who lives? Who dies? and Who decides?

Who decides? That question, the particular concern of this section, touches on one of the most difficult bioethical areas. What happens in such a situation is a variation of a medical practice well known in wartime and in instances of disaster during peacetime. In general, a hard choice is made on the basis of where the application of scarce resources will do the most good. In war and disaster the determination seems less difficult, at least to those safely out of range of responsibility. Someone has to decide, quickly, and giving orders and accepting decisions seem part of a necessary regimen, born of an emergency.

English has borrowed a French word, *triage,* to specify such a system of determination. Originally the term was strictly a product of battlefield conditions. Somehow, society inherently recoils at the idea of adapting battlefield, or lifeboat, ethics to more normal times. The need for making such choices often arises, however, and in the first extract in this section, from the book *Muted Consent,* Jan Wojcik of Purdue University discusses the problems posed by the choices and relates them to the whole area of public health.

Related health issues are experimentation on human

subjects and organ transplants, problems fraught with thorny ethical, medical, and legal questions, and not solely for Americans: the "automatic transplant" became in 1978 a big issue in France; suddenly the rank-and-file citizen became aware of a new law that had made his or her body part of a national bank of hearts, kidneys, livers, eyes, and the like, which could be transplanted in bodies of persons needing them. Such a transplant could be performed automatically unless the potential donor or the donor's family members had forbidden the action in advance.

The creation, in 1974, of a national commission to protect subjects of biomedical and behavioral research projects is the most concrete evidence of national concern over such experimentation in the United States. Informed consent of the participants, and information on compensation for possible injury, became mandatory in 1979. Left very much up in the air was the matter of who should pay the damages, and on what scale and for how long. If the federal government sponsors research conducted by a private university, what is the liability, if any, of the person in charge of the experimentation?

That there is a strong trend toward federal regulation of such activity, difficult as it may be to administer, is a source of gratification to bioethicists. Particular attention has been paid to the protection of children and also of inmates of prisons, long considered suitable subjects of experiments with drugs. Federal guidelines have been established in most areas of human research, and they are constantly under review. Yet another side of the matter is the danger that ethical concerns may blot out recognition of the need for research in general, a need that is stressed by many scientists. Just as ecological considerations must be balanced against economic realities, so must bioethics be recognized as a safeguard against science, not as its unalterable foe.

Especially in behavioral research, much has been made of the individual right of privacy and of the seeming underhandedness of such experiments as those often conducted by federal intelligence and defense agencies. In a way, the criticisms recall the famous words of Justice Oliver Wendell Holmes in the pioneer (1928) Supreme Court case involving the admission of evidence gained by wiretapping: such dirty business. Whether the intelligence-defense experiments should be viewed strictly in that light, or as part of practice prompted by the business of surviving in an admittedly imperfect world, is a theme suggested by the second selection, from *Psychology Today*. The author, Perry London, a behavioral psychologist at the University of Southern California, makes clear the need for a watchdog.

The next two articles in this section deal with forms of behavior modification. Although the potential hazards of work in recombinant DNA are perhaps more frightening than those of psychological engineering, the behavior modifiers are viewed with a particular wariness; whereas the DNA danger seems of mass dimensions, the perils of the other field appear directed especially toward the individual as human guinea pig, and George Orwell seems to caution us as 1984 approaches. In the first of these selections on behavioral modification (another excerpt from *Muted Consent*), Jan Wojcik discusses psychotropic drugs (including so-called mood and anti-anxiety medications) and forms of brain surgery, notably psychosurgery, the goal of which is not so much curative as creative: to transform the subject into a *different* person. The bioethical implications are readily apparent. In the following selection, from *Science News*, Joel Greenberg, the journal's behavioral sciences editor, concentrates on psychosurgery. The article followed shortly after a controversial 1977 report by a national commission. A later report still contained no final judgment on safety or efficacy, but noted some benefits. The debate goes on, and in that respect, the subject resembles virtually every other considered in this book.

The concluding extract, taken from the journal *Philosophy & Public Affairs*, is a discussion of policies regarding the transplantation of cadaver organs. The author,

James L. Muyskens, is a professor of philosophy and well-known commentator on bioethical questions.

ALLOCATION OF SCARCE MEDICAL RESOURCES [1]

. . . Health needs are limitless—everybody saved from a deadly infection by an antibiotic lives to be vulnerable to accidents or chronic sickness or the diseases of old age—while medical resources are limited. Every dollar given to purchase military armaments or a city park could have been spent on a public health clinic. Every dollar a citizen gives in taxes he or she could have used to purchase more sophisticated medical treatment at home.

Two obvious questions arise from the discrepancy between limitless needs and limited means. One is how are we to decide who gets what is available when there isn't enough to go around? Are only the rich to be healthy? Even if they are, what if two of them compete for the same scarce life-saving medical resource, for example, a dialysis machine? The recently published *Burton Report* estimated that it would cost $701 million to buy and maintain enough machines to service the fifty thousand patients who develop endstage kidney disease each year in this country. It would cost $1.043 billion by the fifth year of the program, between $1.816 and $2.702 billion by the fifteenth. The report recommended that the number of patients be winnowed to six to eight thousand a year (selecting the most ideal patients) to make the programs more economically feasible. The solution to the problem of how to select these patients could be used to allocate heart-lung machines, organs available for transplants, inoculations, dental care, and all other scarce resources.

[1] From the book, *Muted Consent: A Casebook in Modern Medical Ethics*, by Jan Wojcik, Purdue University English Department. Chapter 6, p 118-27. Copyright © 1978 by the Purdue Research Foundation, West Lafayette, Indiana, U.S.A.

Another question, perhaps a more basic one, is what should be made available in the first place? How much should a society spend on medicine? How big a piece of the pie should be cut for building dialysis machines, funding cancer research, or immunizing a whole population against preventable diseases like measles and polio? In this chapter, we consider responses to each question in turn.

Allocation of Scarce Supplies

Writers have suggested three ways to allocate scarce available medical resources among the needy—for example, a kidney donated by a dying patient: select patients for care according to their relative worth, select them blindly by lottery, or select no one at all and let *everyone* suffer. Edmond Cahn [*The Moral Decision*, '55] finds the idea of using a lottery to decide human life so repugnant that he argues if not all can be saved then none should be saved. A crisis in human lives "involves stakes too high for gambling and responsibilities too deep for destiny," he says while discussing the legal case often cited as having the most implications for this problem of medical ethics (although the circumstances were quite different). In *United States* v. *Holmes*, the defendant, a ship's mate in charge of a lifeboat after his ship had sunk, was charged with manslaughter for his decision to throw overboard fourteen male passengers to lighten the boat. The judge, in charging the jury, said that if the sailors on the lifeboat had been indispensable for navigation, then the victims to be sacrificed among the passengers should have been chosen by lot so that there would have been no covert discrimination among them. Human beings have equal worth when any must be selected for doom. According to Cahn, the situation in the lifeboat or in a hospital short of medical resources requires that individual human beings declare themselves willing to sacrifice themselves. If insufficient numbers of free volunteers come forth, then the community which fails to produce its own heroes condemns itself to an equal death for all.

Leo Shatin [*American Journal of Orthopsychiatry*, '67], on the other hand, thinks that a community could make decisions less drastically. He reasons that as there is no way to escape making value judgments about who is more deserving in a crisis situation; the criteria to be applied in selection should at least be made explicit and open to argument and adjustment. Polls of public opinion could establish criteria according to profession (clergy rated higher than businessmen, for example) and according to functions in the community (mothers rated higher than spinsters). He rejects the notion of a process of random selection because it would often reward "socially disvalued qualities by giving their bearers the same medical care opportunities as those received by the bearers of socially valued qualities."

Using Social Worth for Patient Selection

In 1961, Dr. Belding H. Scribner set up a program guided by principles similar to those Shatin has in mind in order to screen patients at the Swedish Hospital in Seattle, Washington, for hemodialysis treatment. The Admissions and Policies Committee of the Seattle Artificial Kidney Center at Swedish Hospital was comprised of a lawyer, a clergyman, a housewife, a banker, a labor leader, and two physicians, all of whom remained anonymous to the public, the patients, and the members of the hospital staff. They were commissioned to set their own guidelines and to apply them. The only advice physicians gave them was to reject automatically children who hadn't reached puberty (treatment slows or prevents puberty because children often don't have the stamina for the treatment regimen) or adults over forty-five (whose bodies are more prone to develop serious complications).

The committee decided to base its decisions on criteria of social worth. Patients were accepted or rejected on the basis of how much education they had, how easy it would be for their spouses to remarry, how active they were in church work. Although both the patients and the committee approved of the committee's work, both groups agonized over the procedure. A patient who was chosen to live said, "What a dreadful decision! It's like trying to play God. Frankly, I'm surprised the doctors were able to round up seven people who were willing to take the job." The banker on the committee said, "I've never had any idea how a kidney works, and I still don't. But I do have reservations about the moral aspects of the propriety of choosing A and not B, for whatever reason. I have often asked myself, as a human being, do I have that right? I don't really think I do. I finally came to the conclusion that we are not making a moral choice here. We are picking guinea pigs for experimental purposes. This happens to be true; it also happens to be the way I rationalize my presence on this committee." One of the physicians said, "Being a medical man, I sometimes hear it via the grapevine when a patient whom we have passed over dies. Each time this happens there always comes a feeling of deep regret—perhaps we chose the wrong man. One can just never face these situations without feeling a little sick inside" [Shana Alexander, *Life,* N. 9, '62].

The author of the article from which these quotations were taken felt uncomfortable not so much with the fact that decisions had to be made as with the criteria for selection. "On the basis of the past year's record, a candidate who plans to come before this committee would seem well-advised to father a great many children, then to throw away all his money, and finally to fall ill in a season when there will be a minimum of competition from other men dying of the same disease." David Sanders and Jesse Dukeminier who studied the committee's work were more explicit in their criticism of a procedure that turned middle-class values into criteria for deciding who would live. They find "a disturbing picture of the bourgeoisie sparing the bourgeoisie. . . . The Pacific Northwest is not the place for a Henry David Thoreau with bad kidneys" [*UCLA Law Review,* F. '68].

Using a Lottery for Patient Selection

The Holmes case and the Seattle committee loom large in the thinking of other writers who favor a lottery for its random disregard of volatile moral evaluations. "Randomness as a moral principle" writes Paul Freund, "deserves serious study" [*Daedalus,* Spr. '69]. Paul Ramsey points up a disturbing logical consequence to selecting patients on the basis of their social worth. What if a patient's morals degenerate and he or she starts to carouse and run around or gets divorced while on dialysis; should such a patient be dropped from the program so that a position could be offered to someone else more sober? [Ramsey, *The Patient As Person,* '70.] For the same reasons that Sanders and Dukeminier state, he feels uncomfortable with the use of middle-class standards for judging a person worthy to live. He also concurs with another argument in their study that shifting the onus of evaluation to a physician or a psychiatrist would simply be shifting the same kind of criteria into other hands. Medical suitability is often "doctored" to suit a person's social worth. He also rejects as too severe Cahn's argument that if no one volunteers to sacrifice himself, all should die.

Ramsey favors using a lottery. Its use acknowledges each patient's equal right to treatment and gives each an equal opportunity to get it. He suggests that the process have three stages: First, rules could be announced in advance which are not discriminatory, but based on statistical medical probabilities. Children under the age of puberty and adults over forty-five are bad risks for dialysis. Secondly, dialysis machines could be assigned on a first-come, first-served basis. The applicant with the most seniority whose health was still unimpaired enough for treatment would automatically be granted a place on a suddenly vacant machine. Third, lots could be cast. All three methods could be used separately or in sequence until selection was made. . . .

Ramsey adopts one qualification to this process from

Paul Freund: When a group of human beings are reduced to needing "focused criteria" to survive, they can choose among themselves according to their immediate social value. Freund cites the decision made in North Africa in World War II to use scarce supplies of penicillin to cure syphilis rather than serious war wounds. The men wounded in brothels could be more quickly returned to the front than those wounded in battle.

A similar exception could be made when a disaster such as an earthquake or an aerial bomb strikes a large population at once and wounds far more people than there are medical supplies to treat, creating a need for a system of triage. The survivors are divided into three groups. Those seriously wounded with little hope of recovery receive no treatment; hopeless cases, they are left to die without being allowed to consume any precious resources. Those only slightly injured who can function without medication also receive no treatment. They are assumed able to help in attending to the third or middle group: wounded persons who, if treated, could recover sufficiently to help in the rescue and rebuilding operations. Perhaps even slightly wounded physicians would be treated if this enabled them to better serve the whole group.

Systematic Selection

James F. Childress, after reviewing most of the literature mentioned here, chooses a more systematic procedure of random selection [*Soundings,* Winter '70]. First, the patient group should be screened objectively by doctors using medical criteria, automatically rejecting people not acceptable for reasons of age or their suffering from other diseases. These criteria should be broad lest there develop a process of "fine comparison" at this stage—rejecting one patient because he is slightly older or slightly less healthy looking than another. If after this selection there are still more applicants than resources, a lottery should choose among them. This process is a fair way, Childress thinks, for granting equal rights to all human beings in the face

of inadequate medical supplies and the limited capacity
of individual human beings for altruism.

Frederic B. Westervelt, Jr., M.D., replies to Childress
and through him to Ramsey and Freund by criticizing the
lottery method [*Soundings,* Winter '70]. He argues that it
operates under false pretenses in that it does not really
disregard patients' social worth. Primarily upper- and
middle-class people are fortunate enough to enjoy early
diagnosis of their ills. Consequently, he reasons, only they
get a shot at scarce resources. Discrimination has already
occurred in pre-selection. From another tack, Westervelt
asks what if a doctor decides that a patient with an ailing
kidney could be treated with drugs and diet for a long time
before any need for dialysis arose. Would this patient lose
his or her place in the "first-come, first-served" line when
dialysis became necessary just because some less-scarce
remedy worked for a time? What if a patient selected by a
lottery was cantankerous and would not get along well
with the doctors or lived too far from the dialysis center
to be able to meet regular appointments? Should patients
such as these be replaced by more polite, more reasonable,
or more accessible patients?

Westervelt finally argues that a system of triage should
be applied by a physician who takes into account the
patient's morale, health, and convenience, as well as his
or her social worth. Someone should be willing to take the
moral responsibility for the decision. . . .

Choosing Among Medical Programs

Some writers who take up the second question of what
medical resources should be made available in the first
place throw up their hands in despair. Ramsey writes that
". . . the question of setting priorities, which—tragically,
perhaps—must be faced and thought through by the medical
profession and by society in general . . . is a question that
is almost if not altogether incorrigible to rational determination" [*The Patient As Person,* '70]. . . . After an

extensive review of the literature on the subject, Henry Beecher writes: "It was a considerable disappointment to the writer, after the examination of more than a dozen areas where scarce resources were involved, to find statements of only the most rudimentary principles of procedure" [*Daedalus*, Spr. '69].

Beecher's study of the manifold causes of scarcity emphasizes the dilemma. He begins with a history of the development of certain medical techniques such as anesthesia, insulin, penicillin and the Chamberlen forceps for aiding difficult child delivery. All were scarce at the beginning because they were untested and not yet widely reproduced, but they stayed scarce for different lengths of time for very different reasons. The Chamberlen family kept their discovery secret for many years in order to sell it privately for high prices. It could have been easily imitated and widely distributed. William Thomas Green Morton kept secret the active agents of his "Lethon" used as an anesthesia because he felt careful experimentation was necessary before its use became widespread. Public pressure finally forced him to reveal the components and to distribute the resource. Penicillin was initially a scarce resource because it could not be produced fast enough to meet the many demands for it. The use of insulin developed slowly as it was experimentally given only to severe cases until the proper dosages and the possible side effects were determined. Avarice, rudimentary production, or caution can cause scarcity.

Other kinds of human attitudes also play a part. In certain states there is a prejudice against using "racially mixed" blood. All fresh blood and blood plasma must be designated according to the race of its donor so that a squeamish patient might refuse it. This could radically restrict the amount of blood available to a particular patient at a certain time. Jehovah's Witnesses voluntarily limit the medical resources available to them when they refuse all blood transfusions on religious principles. Ameri-

can Navy men in the eighteenth and nineteenth centuries
suffered from scurvy because of their ignorance of or prejudice against the successful British practice of putting limes
in the diet of British Navy men as a prophylactic. There
are finally ethical restraints against using certain resources
which, as a result, become scarce. The Uniform Anatomical
Gift Act stipulates that only donor-volunteered organs can
be used in transplant surgery. Similar restraints against
experimentation with children, prisoners, or unconsenting
human subjects likewise retard the development of medical
technology.

Finally, Beecher points to the inertia of medical research itself. Christiaan Barnard's spectacular early success
with heart transplants attracted to his transplant research
a lot of money which thereby became less available for other
medical programs. Cancer research likewise absorbs the
money that could be used to inoculate children in rural
areas or in Third World countries against measles, polio,
and other controllable diseases. Politics plays a role as well.
Well-to-do white people are perhaps more interested in
the diseases that threaten them such as cancer and, consequently, support research in these areas more strongly.
Sickle-cell anemia research and treatment began to advance
much more rapidly after black political groups began to
publicize their problems and solicit support.

When Ramsey purviews the politics of medical distribution, he finds himself perplexed and loath to make any
principled decision to favor one kind of medicine over
another: "A civilization consists of many different qualities
and levels of activities as does medical practice. In the
recovery of Europe after World War II, opera houses were
rebuilt along with housing for the homeless" [*The Patient
As Person*, '70].

[Gerald] Leach draws out several hidden paradoxes in
the muddle. Mass prevention campaigns against infectious
diseases usually wind up *increasing* medical costs. Prevention costs more than the treatment of the few who used to
get the disease. Likewise "the cost of screening everybody

could still be much higher than the conventional approach of letting these diseases take hold and trying to cure the few advanced cases that one can" [*The Biocrats,* '70]. As great numbers of the population become immune to curable diseases, their medical needs rise in sophistication. Soon everyone who survives polio, the measles, diabetes, and so forth, will be threatened only by cancer and beyond that death itself. The principle at work here is that as "the standards of what it means to be 'healthy' rise . . . the total of reported illness actually rises" [*The Biocrats,* '70]. Those who finally reach this plateau will probably be grateful if, while they were being inoculated, sophisticated research against the disease that now threatens them was being carried on continuously.

If one follows the reasoning of Ramsey and Leach there would seem to be no way out of the dilemma of inequitable distribution. There is no way to weigh conflicting needs against each other, and even if there were, one need would eventually replace the other. Perhaps there is a certain amount of comfort that can be taken from all this. Perhaps something like Adam Smith's "invisible hand" directing the economic market directs the medical market as well. Perhaps society as a whole is making decisions about the advancement of medicine or the distribution of resources through a process of balancing conflicting interests. On this level the process is immune to meddling or resistent to programming, depending on your point of view; no "system" would distribute goods any better than the current free market does. One could take comfort in hoping that the society is serving its own best interests far better than any direct political control of the process could. *Laissez-faire* could be letting a fundamentally benign process go its cautious, merry way.

EXPERIMENTS ON HUMANS [2]

When it was discovered that the CIA was secretly giving psychedelic drugs to unsuspecting Americans for many years, a wave of revulsion swept the country. The psychological dynamics underlying our anger had less to do with law than with two principles that are built into the ideological consciousness of Americans from childhood on —first, that you should not push people around; second, that sneaks are scoundrels and sneaky behavior is rotten behavior. These attitudes had been instrumental, until World War II, in preventing the U.S. from having an extensive intelligence service at all. In violating them since, the CIA confirmed our worst fears of what an undercover agency might do.

The same abhorrence of bullies and sneaks produced the psychological impetus for the principle of *informed* consent, which has become a major point of professional ethics in the last couple of decades and probably will soon be a matter of law everywhere in this country. Informed consent means that someone gives you permission in advance to do something to them, and that they know what you are going to do when they agree to it. But agreement alone is not enough. You must be certain that their consent is intelligently given, based on their full understanding of what is involved in your proposal and of the risks that may be connected with it. Getting consent without giving information is seduction, that is, trickery.

It is easy to see the dangers to a free society when its already secret agencies start compounding their cloak-and-dagger operations with experiments such as those conducted by the CIA. The need for informed consent, however, and

[2] Article entitled "Experiments on Humans: Where to Draw the Line," by Perry London, professor of psychology and psychiatry, University of California. *Psychology Today.* v 11, no 6, p 20-3. N. '77. Reprinted from Psychology Today Magazine. Copyright © 1977 Ziff-Davis Publishing Company.

the dangerous implications of not getting it, is just as great in other situations that have nothing to do with national security. The most important area of concern, in this connection, is biomedical research, ranging from cancer to social psychology.

In 1963, some cancer researchers in Brooklyn, New York, injected live cancer cells into some old people to see if they would "take." The scientists were pretty sure they would not, but, just in case, they did not tell the subjects what the injections were or why they were giving them. "We didn't want to worry them," was the explanation later offered to a Congressional investigating committee. The scientists did not, incidentally, try the injections on themselves because, as one of them put it, he thought he was "too valuable" to the project. The old people were told they were getting injections of some "cell suspension," and they consented to them, probably thinking they were getting some kind of medicine. They were misinformed here for the purpose of deceiving them.

If the scientists in that study had had a sharper sense of ethics, they would have known not only that it was wrong to misinform people as they did, but also that they could have gotten plenty of volunteer subjects by explaining just what the experiment was about, what its risks were, and what benefits to humanity might have resulted by being part of it. There are many adventurous and altruistic people who are eager to participate in all kinds of experiments.

Even the most ethically refined scientists, however, cannot deal so easily with situations where a lack of information, or downright deception, is a central requirement of the experiment. In some important drug research and social-psychology studies, for instance, giving subjects advance information about all aspects of the experiment could bias their responses to it in ways that might make the results meaningless. In some studies, in fact, even letting people know that there is an experiment going on and that they are subjects in it might ruin the outcome.

Experiments with new drugs, especially drugs that affect

people's mental states, like tranquilizers or stimulants, illustrate the problem. Here, it is important to separate the chemical effects of the drugs from their "placebo" effects, that is, the psychological effects that simply taking a pill may have on people who know what it is supposed to do to them. The only way to sort out the purely psychological effects is to give, for example, some people a placebo and see how they respond to it, and perhaps give other people the real drug without telling them what it is supposed to do. There is no way to do such experiments and still get completely informed consent from the subjects. The more you tell them about the drugs and the experiment, the more you weaken the significance of its results. But, at the same time, the more risk there is in taking a new drug, the more clearly obligated you are to tell people what you are doing.

The social and behavioral sciences present equally great problems with informed consent. The two most dramatic illustrations come from the field of social psychology. In one, a series of experiments on compliance conducted at Yale by Stanley Milgram, it was necessary to lie to the subjects about both the purpose of the experiment and their true role in it. In Milgram's studies, subjects were misled into believing that they were administering severe electric shocks to other subjects, but the shock apparatus was actually not real, and the ostensible victims were really stooges of the experimenter and were not being shocked at all. None of the subjects knew this, and 75 percent of them obeyed orders even though they thought they were inflicting severe damage.

In the other example, experiments by John Darley of Princeton and Bibb Latané of Ohio State, the subjects could not even be told they were participating in the experiment. They were sitting in a waiting room to be called into an experiment when they suddenly heard someone nearby calling urgently for help. Unknown to them, that was the real experiment—its object was to see whether they would respond to such cries (most did not, incidentally, especially if there were other "bystanders" around!).

In both sets of experiments, no one was physically at risk, of course, but critics, particularly of Milgram, argue that psychological damage may have been done to subjects who thought they had acted terribly toward other people. In these, as in all deception studies, the experimenters took pains afterward to "debrief" the subjects, that is, to tell them what the study was really about and to reassure them that they had not misbehaved—but there is some convincing evidence that such debriefings do not work very well. The result is that some critics think deception studies should not be done at all.

Were they not to be done, on the other hand, some potentially vital information might be lost to both medicine and behavioral science. It is sometimes possible to bypass deception and "noninforming" designs to get valid experimental results, but where these designs are crucial, as in Milgram-type studies, the stark choice before ethical scientists is to abandon the experiment or abandon the desired information. There are plenty of glib answers offered by cavalier ethicists—that informed consent is more important than any scientific considerations; and by insensitive researchers—that seeking valuable scientific information makes it all right to deceive subjects or put them at risk. But neither extreme position will do for those of us who are equally concerned with the need for valid scientific information and for the protection of human subjects.

As the tension between these needs becomes more apparent, discussion of the issues is leaving the area of individual or professional ethical concerns and becoming a matter of law. In 1974, Congress created a National Commission for the Protection of Human Subjects of Biomedical and Behavioral Research. It was assigned to conduct studies of the ethical issues surrounding research on human subjects and to devise guidelines and make recommendations that could be incorporated into the codes of conduct of granting agencies and the laws of the land.

As a condition of receiving federal support, HEW now requires every research institution to set up a committee to assess in advance the ethical issues in all experiments. HEW also provides some guidelines for the protection of human subjects; for instance, it requires that test subjects must be given "a description of the attendant discomforts and risks" in an experiment, as well as "an offer to answer any inquiries concerning the procedures."

These guidelines offer no clues as to when some amount of deception may be necessary and proper. There are a few general "rules of thumb," however, which individual researchers can use to help answer their personal questions about what are decent boundary lines. It is better, for instance, on practical as well as ethical grounds, to inform people fully about your experimental intentions because it reduces the number of things that can go wrong by inadvertent misinformation. Silence is sometimes necessary in experiments, and so is deception, but they are never desirable if they can be done without. Experimenters must always ask three questions before using deception or noninforming designs: Is there any way to get valid information without such practice? Is the information to be gained so valuable that it is worth the trouble of misleading, debriefing, and apologizing, which may be necessary? Is there significant risk of damaging subjects' feelings, so that merely telling them the truth afterward will not correct the harm —or may even make it worse by adding the humiliation of making them feel they were "taken"?

It is clear that there was far too much deceptive research going on in the past. But it is also clear that some of it will have to be done in the future. The less, the better seems to be the most ethical and practical principle, but when more scientists sensitize themselves to these issues, perhaps we can all define where the line should be drawn more carefully.

BEHAVIOR CONTROL [3]

Recently developed behavior-control technology has made spectacular advances in treating mental disabilities, from MBD—minimal brain dysfunction, most often called hyperactivity syndrome—to the involuntary homicidal rages of certain types of epileptics. In 1937 it was discovered that doses of amphetamines which can excite adults seem paradoxically to calm hyperkinetic (hyperactive) children. These children often run around like human dynamos, act up in classrooms, and find it difficult to pay attention to anything for an extended period of time. The drug seems to "stimulate" greater restraint which can have a domino effect on the child's behavior. As the child becomes more attentive, he wins more praise for his work and finds it easier to get along with other children. Self-esteem increases. When the drug was used with the more difficult children in an institution for delinquent children, all the children became more manageable.

Since World War II, the development and administration of other psychotropic drugs, those which influence the mind and alter behavior, mood, and mental functioning, such as antipsychotics (tranquilizers) antidepressants (amphetamines) , and antianxiety drugs (Librium, Valium, and so forth) , have had a dramatic impact on the treatment of mental diseases in adults. The drugs seem to balance chemical instability in the brain, making it possible for a patient to lead a more normal life in the face of otherwise unbearable stress. More patients can be treated at home, where there is more free space and less violence than in hospitals. The stigma attached to mental illness has lessened. Patients can adjust to their normal life situations more easily.

[3] From the book, *Muted Consent: A Casebook in Modern Medical Ethics*, by Jan Wojcik, Purdue University English Department. Chapter 4, p 68-72. Copyright © 1978 by the Purdue Research Foundation, West Lafayette, Indiana.

Since the 1940s and mostly under the influence of B. F. Skinner, a Harvard psychologist and behaviorist, techniques of behavior modification have become very sophisticated. Pavlov's earlier experiments in conditioning a dog to respond to artificial stimulus associated with a natural stimulus (salivating to the sound of a bell that was rung many times while meat was being presented) have led to the development of operant conditioning—changing the reinforcements of a behavior in order to change the behavior. A smug inmate of a mental institution who does no work and yet is fed anyway is told that from now on only work will earn food. Doing no work (the undesired behavior) now leads to no food (a new negative reinforcement); working (the desired behavior) leads to food (a new positive reinforcement). An American psychiatrist, Lloyd H. Cotter, described the effect operant conditioning had on a Vietnamese mental hospital during the war. When he arrived in 1966, he found the hospital with very poor morale, with diminishing stores of food and drugs. He decided to attack the problems of lassitude and lack of food simultaneously. Patients were told they had to work if they ever hoped to be discharged. A small number volunteered. Those who refused were immediately given unmodified electro-convulsive treatments on a regular basis. After some weeks, many were helped by the treatment; others improved greatly when, through dislike of the treatment, they joined the work force.

Later Cotter changed his tactics by adding another reinforcement. He told the patients still not working that if they didn't do some work, they wouldn't be fed. After three days, almost all of the patients were working. . . . Similar techniques have been used to toilet train seriously disturbed children, and to teach them to interrelate with other people and even to speak and read.

In the early 1950s, James Olds inspired an enormous amount of research into techniques for exploring and changing the brain when he implanted an electrode into the brain of a rat and found he could alter its behavior and mood by switching the current on and off. The therapeutic psychosurgery which has developed—lobotomy, electric stimulation of the brain (ESB), and other techniques that cut or coagulate with electrical current parts of the brain —has enabled doctors to blunt tension and anxiety, and to control violence in patients who don't respond to either drugs or psychological conditioning. In the process the surgeons have attracted sharp ethical questioning by their presumption to cure sickness by changing the patient permanently—not into a healthy person which not even conventional medicine can presume to do—but into a different person. Even before the electrical probe or knife touches the target area of the operation, it has cut through a delicate structure of neurological relays that eons of human evolution and perhaps decades of personal experience have shaped. Psychosurgery, probably more than any other branch of medicine, is developing a formative rather than curative science.

In 1970, two neurosurgeons, Vernon H. Mark and Frank R. Ervin, reported the case of a patient, Thomas, an epileptic with a history of seizures and episodes of uncontrollable, murderous rages. He would suddenly and without provocation try to harm members of his family. It was determined that certain types of epileptic electrical activity triggered the rages even at times when there was no overt indication that a seizure was taking place or imminent. He did not respond to treatment with psychotropic drugs.

The surgeons inserted electrodes into Thomas's brain which they could use to stimulate different parts of his brain in order to discover which part, when stimulated, brought on the symptoms of one of his rages. For three months they kept him free of rages through the electrical stimulation of his relaxation mood whenever he appeared about to fall into his mood of anger. After this period of observation they determined that, having located the diseased part of the brain with certitude, it was time to operate to neutralize it, to make the patient's therapy permanent. After stimulating him to relax, they asked his consent. He agreed and was happy with his decision until the effects of his stimulation faded, at which point he "turned wild and unmanageable," absolutely refusing any further therapy. Only after several weeks of patient explanation were the doctors able to convince Thomas to have the lesion of his brain made. "Four years have passed since the operation, during which time Thomas has not had a single episode of rage" [Mark and Ervin, *Violence in the Brain*, '70].

Lobotomy, a lesion along the midline base of the frontal lobe, treats more generalized unmanageability. At first, in the 1950s, it was widely used in this country to sedate chronically ill patients in mental institutions. Some fifty thousand operations were performed. More recently it has been used to treat hyperactive children and neurotics. An Indian, Dr. Balasubraminian, reporting his results with 115 patients (three of them under the age of five, thirty-six under eleven), indicates why it was and is again becoming popular: "The improvement that occurs has been remarkable. In one case a patient had been assaulting his colleagues and the ward doctors; after the operation he became a helpful addition to the ward staff and looked after other patients."

A German experimenter, F. D. Roeder, recently made lesions in the hypothalamic region to cure a patient of sexually deviant behavior. In his report he writes, "Potency was weakened, but preserved. . . . The aberrant sexuality of this patient was considerably suppressed, without serious side effects. The important feature was the patient's incapacity of indulging in erotic fancies and stimulating visions" [Breggin, *Quality of Health Care*, '73].

All three forms of behavior control work to shape the "will" of a person, a philosophic term for the control a person exercises over his or her behavior. It is easy to see how it could be used for the good of a patient like Thomas —who might be better able to control embarrassing, inefficient, or self-destructive impulses—and for the good of his family and society at large. Restrained personalities are easier for everyone to live with. At the same time, it is easy to see how behavior control could be used for ill, especially if the physician deciding what inadequate self-control is and what adequate medical controls are doesn't share the views of either the patient or other members of the society. The American doctor, Cotter, for example, doesn't consider it important to determine whether his Vietnamese inmates' attitudes towards work might be shaped by their very different culture or their experiences in the war. According to his report, his decision to change their habitual behavior seemed to be even to them the right one. The problem is perhaps more acute when patients are unruly rather than too passive. How well could a physician draw the line between erratic social behavior and radical social action, between a patient who disrupts the order of a hospital because he is sick and tired of an injustice he perceives there, or another who disrupts it because he is just sick?

PSYCHOSURGERY AT THE CROSSROADS [4]

The fact that psychosurgery's effect on the brain is unknown doesn't make it a distinctive treatment in our society—Allan F. Mirsky, neuropsychologist, Boston University.

Egas Moniz had heard reports that cutting the brain's frontal lobe had a calming effect on monkeys and chimpanzees. So, in 1935, the Portuguese neuropsychiatrist began operating on the frontal lobes of his psychiatric patients. In a monograph, Moniz described generally favorable results on his first 20 patients, and he encouraged colleagues around the world to adopt similar procedures.

Less than a year later, neurologist Walter Freeman and neurosurgeon James Watts introduced lobotomies to the

[4] Article by Joel Greenberg, behavioral sciences editor. *Science News.* v 111, no 20, p 314-17. My. 14, '77. Reprinted with permission from SCIENCE NEWS, the weekly news magazine of science, copyright 1977 by Science Service, Inc.

United States. By 1950, the team had operated on more than 1,000 patients, and Freeman estimated that by the time he retired shortly thereafter he had performed or supervised psychosurgical procedures on more than 3,500 individuals.

Today, even though more than 40,000 lobotomies and various updated forms of psychosurgery have been performed in the United States since World War II—and surgeons currently do more than 400 procedures a year in the United States—significantly little has been learned about how and why psychosurgery alters behavior. Indeed, there continues to be heated, at times bitter, disagreement over the surgery's effects, benefits and risks. Proponents contend the procedure works for severely disturbed persons who have tried just about every other form of therapy without success. Critics warn that the surgery is not only "irreversible," but that cutting into the brain carries far more ethical implications than operating on a kidney, intestine or heart, and should be severely limited, if not banned.

It is against this backdrop that the National Commission for the Protection of Human Subjects of Biomedical and Behavioral Research has come out with proposals for the country's first set of formal guidelines governing the use of psychosurgery. The commission defines psychosurgery as "brain surgery on (1) normal brain tissue, or (2) diseased brain tissue of an individual, if the primary object of such surgery is to control, change or affect any behavioral or emotional disturbance of such individual."

The recommendations, released in mid-March [1977], have already heightened the psychosurgery controversy to its most heated point since the beginning of the decade. It was then that the resurgence of psychosurgery reached its peak, after about 10 years when almost no such operations were performed because of feared side effects and the popularity of new, psychoactive drugs. In the mid- to late-1960s, however, surgeons began reporting that certain psychiatric symptoms could be alleviated with more refined and localized cutting techniques. Since then, psychosurgery has settled into a sort of intermediate ground—it is used more than infrequently, but not nearly as often or indiscriminately as in the postwar era.

But even many of its practitioners agree that they are dealing with a relatively radical and mysterious procedure that cries for some form of regulation, or at least direction. The commission, created in 1974 by legislation, contracted with research teams at Boston University and the Massachusetts Institute of Technology to help determine the effectiveness and safety of psychosurgery. The two groups performed follow-up studies on more than 60 persons who had undergone at least one psychosurgical procedure, most during the past 10 years. In addition, University of Michigan psychologist Elliot Valenstein was contracted to perform a literature survey of the extent of psychosurgery in the United States in recent years.

On the basis of those studies—criticized by some as woefully incomplete but nonetheless probably the most comprehensive assessment of psychosurgery thus far—the commission recommended:

Psychosurgery should be performed only at an institution with an HEW-appointed review board, and only after that board has determined that the surgeon is competent; the surgery is appropriate; adequate pre- and postoperative evaluations will be performed; and the patient has given informed consent.

—If the patient is incapable of giving informed consent, it may be obtained from a guardian, if the patient does not object *and* a court in which the patient had legal representation has approved the operation.

—Given the above conditions, psychosurgery may be performed on a voluntary patient at a mental institution, providing a national psychosurgery advisory board has determined that the specific procedure will be of demonstrable benefit to the patient. Similar conditions apply to prisoners and involuntary mental patients and children. Such operations may be performed as part of a research project if certain conditions, specified by the commission, are met.

—The secretary of HEW "is encouraged to conduct and

support studies" to evaluate psychosurgery research. The secretary should impose strict sanctions to assure compliance with the recommendations. Congress should also take legislative action to assure compliance.

The proposals have sparked disagreement both within and outside of the commission. Dissenting commission member Patricia A. King says the recommendations fail to guarantee proper safeguards for voluntary patients by not requiring court review of their cases prior to surgery. She also agrees that outside critics may have some basis for labeling the commission's "encouragement" of HEW support a blanket endorsement of psychosurgery.

Longtime critics such as Washington, D.C., psychiatrist Peter Breggin have called the commission's report a "whitewash" and charged that its members were biased toward psychosurgery.

But possibly the most thoughtful and searching questions about the report deal with the studies used by the commission to reach its conclusions. Stephen Chorover, an MIT psychologist, perhaps the most articulate critic of psychosurgery, says the commission report "relies too heavily on two studies. The facts are tentative, questionable and incomplete. The commission has placed enormous emphasis . . . on a relatively small proportion of patients over a short period of time."

The MIT study, headed by Hans-Lukas Teuber (who died recently), examined 34 adult patients who had undergone surgical lesions in the brain's anterior cingulate region. (Psychosurgery has progressed from the gross severing of frontal lobes some 30 years ago to smaller, more localized cuts in various regions of the brain.) The patients had problems ranging from pain to depression to obsessive-compulsive behavior to schizophrenia and other emotional problems. Ten of the subjects had experienced more than one psychosurgical operation, including four who had three cingulotomies.

Researchers at MIT said that five of the seven depressed patients reported full or partial relief, but the four obsessive-compulsives remained "quite unrelieved," and the 12 diagnosed with schizophrenia or other illnesses had mixed results. Nine of the 11 patients whose primary symptom was pain, experienced complete or nearly complete relief.

Behaviorally, psychosurgery produced "no significant effects," the researchers reported after administering 24 tests, including verbal, perceptual and IQ measures. After initially scoring lower on some tests within four months after surgery, most of the patients then rebounded to score significantly higher (including IQ) than they did before their operations. Psychosurgery "does not seem to make patients detectably worse," concludes MIT's Suzanne Corkin. "There were no lasting additional deficits. However, this is not to say [that psychosurgery] is the ultimate treatment of mental disease." But the MIT results, she continues, "should lead to more direct and effective treatments."

The Boston University team, directed by neuropsychologists Allan F. Mirsky and Maressa H. Orzack, evaluated 27 patients of three surgeons, each of whom performed a different type of operation: orbital undercutting, where the fibers beneath the orbital portion of the prefrontal area are selectively cut; multiple target surgery, where lesions are made in one or more of the three limbic system areas; and ultrasonic irradiation, where the white matter below the cortex is irradiated.

Mirsky reported that 14 of the 27 patients had "very favorable outcomes, were enthusiastic about surgery and would undergo the operation again under similar circumstances." The remainder of the patients—who, like the MIT subjects, ran the gamut of psychiatric problems—had results ranging from moderate improvement to worsening of their condition. A battery of psychological, neurological, verbal and nonverbal tests yielded no significant differences between those patients and control groups that had not received psychosurgery, Mirsky reported.

Like the MIT group, the Boston researchers found similar improvements in IQ and certain other tests more than four months after surgery. However, an exception was that operated patients had more difficulty than control subjects in shifting from one category to another in the Wisconsin Card Sorting Task—a finding that reflects frontal lobe dysfunction, according to the researchers. Consistent with isolated, previous findings, the Boston study reported that psychosurgery appears to do the greatest good for persons who are severely depressed. The results also indicated that females tend to have more favorable results than males.

Chorover's criticisms center somewhat on the quality of the Boston and MIT work, but more so on the commission's transformation of the "tentative" findings into recommendations, and on the ethical right of doctors to perform a procedure about which very little is known, as compared with other forms of surgery.

Indeed, Mirsky concedes that his findings show "no relationship" between the type or location of a specific operation and the resulting effect upon the patient. But, he adds, "the fact that psychosurgery's effect on the brain is unknown doesn't make it a distinctive treatment in our society." Many treatments, including various drug therapies, "are also unknown," he says. "But fortunately they benefit the patient."

Chorover, however, contends that "the real questions remain unanswered and unaddressed. We continue to deal with complex, interactive patterns of behavior as if we don't know we're liable to make a terrible mistake if we try to localize [such] problems [in the brain].

"The fact that people have problems does not mean it is legitimate to alter their behavior," he says. "I suggest that the [commission's] regulations impede . . . and sidestep the real problems. They substitute procedural guidelines for real solutions." Breggin goes even further, suggesting that such intrusion into the brain constitutes "mutilation" of the sort which is generally prohibited by law.

Both men have voiced deep concern that psychosurgery will be misused as a social or political tool, conveniently employed to subdue the "abnormal" behavior of institutionalized persons, blacks, women or other minorities. (Valenstein's research notes that women comprise 56 percent of all psychosurgery patients, but that other minorities constitute a minute percentage.) Says Chorover: "So long as inequalities of power exist between those who define problems and those who have problems, the power of science and technology may continue to be used . . . in definitions of mental illness."

In a recent head-to-head debate with Chorover at the Eastern Psychological Association meeting in Boston, Mirsky pointed out that psychosurgery presently accounts for only 0.005 percent of all treatment for psychiatric illness. It was also noted that the procedure is done at twice the U.S. rate in Great Britain, and three times the American rate in Australia. The neuropsychologist also addressed several other criticisms of psychosurgery:

—The procedure *is* irreversible, but so are various types of long-term drug treatment.

—Psychosurgery is "never" performed without trying other therapies first. "We find patients who do not benefit from psychotherapy," Mirsky says. "And we see drug treatments that do not work and produce side effects."

—Psychosurgery may be undesirable under some circumstances, but it is not used nearly as often as electroshock therapy, which, Mirsky notes, often produces "bad side effects and prolonged hospitalization." In the MIT study, the 26 patients who had received electric-shock therapy prior to surgery generally were inferior to the remaining 8 subjects on verbal and nonverbal tests. Some of those patients had received more than 100 shock treatments in their lifetimes, according to the MIT report.

Mirsky further points out that if those in the Boston University study who experienced moderate improvement were added to those who were very much improved, the success rate would be 78 percent. Chorover believes such claims are shaky at best, primarily because of the relatively small sample size and the comparatively little knowledge available about psychosurgery as a tool. According to

Valenstein's research, just four surgeons are responsible for 48 percent of the procedures performed in this country. About half of the remaining operations are done by surgeons who perform psychosurgery only about once a year, Valenstein says.

Chorover and others view such statistics as warning flags that psychosurgery is still controlled and understood (as well as it can be) by a relatively few professionals. Such observations have led National Institute of Mental Health Director Bertram S. Brown to favor psychosurgery as experimental, to be conducted only within the context of research, and subject to all the review provisions and procedures available for the protection of human subjects.

Concludes Chorover: "Can these types of problems be dealt with by regulations? The activities of psychosurgery must be viewed within their social context."

CADAVER ORGANS FOR TRANSPLANTATION [5]

Two moral principles have been basic to the legal decisions concerning the rights and duties toward the newly dead. They are the duty to give decent burial and the denial to anyone of a right to ownership of the dead body for commercial profit (for example, a body cannot be sold as security for the payment of a debt). The next-of-kin—rather than the church (as was the case earlier in the West) or the state—have come to bear the primary responsibility for providing decent burial.

The familial duty to give decent burial has come to be understood as a legal right to determine what is to be done to the body in the interval between death and burial. . . .

[5] From article entitled "An Alternative Policy for Obtaining Cadaver Organs for Transplantation," by James L. Muyskens, associate professor and chairman of the Department of Philosophy, Hunter College, City University of New York. *Philosophy & Public Affairs.* v 8, no 1, p 88-99. Fall '78. By permission of the author.

Armed with this right, the family has had the power to deny permission for the use of an organ for transplantation or for the performance of an autopsy. Significantly, however, in certain cases of criminal investigation or the settlement of an insurance contract, an autopsy may be performed on the ground that the interest of society takes precedence over the contrary wishes of the family.

In addition to the interests of society and of the family are the wishes of the deceased (for example, his expressed wish that his body be donated to science or that his body not be cremated). The courts have maintained both that the expressed wish of the deceased ought to be carried out and also that the sentiments of the living should be protected. In cases in which the interests of the living and the wishes of the deceased are in conflict, it has not been clear (until recently) how the courts would exercise their "benevolent discretion."

One of the major aims of the Uniform Anatomical Gift Act proposed in 1968 was to guarantee that the wishes of the deceased—in cases in which she or he has expressed a desire to donate organs for transplantation or to bequeath her or his body to medical authorities for their use—not be revoked by next-of-kin. That is, it was proposed that in cases of conflict, the expressed wishes of the deceased take priority over those of the next-of-kin. However, in cases in which the deceased did not express a desire to donate or have known objections to such donations, the next-of-kin may do so. The basic provisions of the Uniform Anatomical Gift Act are:

1. Any individual over eighteen may give all or part of his body for educational, research, therapeutic, or transplantation purposes.
2. If the individual has not made a donation before his death, his next of kin can make it unless there was a known objection by the deceased.
3. If the individual has made such a gift it cannot be revoked by the relatives.

4. If there is more than one person of the same degree of kinship the gift from relatives shall not be accepted if there is known objection by one of them.

5. The gift can be authorized by a card carried by the individual or by written or recorded verbal communication from a relative.

All fifty states have adopted the provisions of the Uniform Anatomical Gift Act. Hence, in the United States any individual eighteen years of age or over or, "in the absence of actual notice of contrary indications by the decedent," a member of the decedent's family may give all or any part of the decedent's body for purposes of medical or dental education, research, or transplantation.

Despite this unprecedented legislative action bringing about uniformity in law in all fifty states and providing a relatively simple means for obtaining cadaver organs for transplantation, the great need for suitable donors remains. There is no question that patients die who would not have to die if there was not a shortage of donors. . . .

One would be inclined to suspect that disapproval on the part of the public may account for the severe shortage. However, according to a Gallup Poll published in the New York *Times* (17 January 1968) 70 percent of adults in the United States approved the donation of their organs after death. As Gerald Leach says, "If willingness to donate were all, there should be no problems with spare hearts, lungs, livers and kidneys from the dead" [*The Biocrats,* '70]. Unfortunately only a small percentage of those approving of organ transplants have taken the steps to make their own available in the event that they become suitable donors. Further, the pool of potential donors must be vast in order to meet the need, since "only the very rare death provides organs suitable for donation" [Veatch, *Death, Dying . . .* '76].

Both the cause of death and the circumstance of death are crucial to the suitability of organs for transplantation.

The best donors are young persons who die of certain types of injuries: automobile accidents or violence, brain tumors, strokes, cerebral hemorrhage, and other central nervous system lesions. The organs of those who die at an old age or die of cancer, of infection, or of chronic vascular diseases are not suitable for transplantation. Because of damage to the organs, persons who are dead on arrival at the hospital are usually unsuitable donors. In other situations, the time is too short to obtain the required permission or a transplant team is not available at the place of death.

Since one of the fundamental objectives of medical practice is to save lives, and since many more lives could be saved if there were more organs available for transplantation, it is apparent that we should attempt to find a way to secure greater quantities of suitable cadaver organs.

The task of developing an acceptable policy on this matter is difficult because we cannot focus on the need to save lives while ignoring other compelling considerations. In trying to achieve the unquestionably worthy goal of saving lives, one must not violate fundamental duties (for example, a doctor's duty to provide the best care he can for the dying patient in his care) or endanger or diminish other important objectives of society (for example, the preservation of religious freedom and enhancement of respect for life). Certain moral constraints and moral objectives must be considered in devising social policy for securing cadaver organs. Before considering these, let us examine the types of policy possible and some actual policy proposals.

Policies for obtaining cadaver organs can be divided into the general categories of "giving," "taking," "trading," "selling."

(1) Giving of cadaver organs. A number of variations are possible. For example, organs may be
(a) given by the family of the deceased in response to a request for certain organs;

   (b) given by the deceased prior to imminent death
        in response to a general appeal for suitable
        organs.
(2) Routine salvaging of cadaver organs. For example,
     (a) routine removal of any and all useful organs;
     (b) routine removal of certain useful organs.
(3) Trading of cadaver organs. For example, an ex-
     change of credits for organs similar to the blood-
     bank system.
(4) Selling of suitable cadaver organs.

Of these four categories, the last clearly violates the
centuries-old principle that no one is entitled to claim
ownership of a dead body for commercial profit. I am not
aware of any serious advocates of such a claim, and
therefore I shall not discuss it further.

The category of "taking" has obvious advantages when
it comes to obtaining the organs necessary for saving lives.
Few would argue against the efficiency of "taking" organs.
But such a practice could violate certain moral constraints
or duties, could endanger values which must be preserved,
and could undermine important social objectives. . . .

I shall now examine the objections to routine salvaging
in order to determine what competing moral values and
constraints must be taken into account in devising a
morally adequate policy. On the basis of this discussion,
I shall suggest a policy that best satisfies these moral
demands.

Any routine salvaging policy removes the need to obtain premortem consent from the donor or postmortem
consent from the family. Clearly, as [Paul] Ramsey states,
such policies place the burden of action on those who, for
whatever reason, object to the removal of organs for
transplantation. Contrary to the other types of policy,
inaction on the part of the donor or the family is not a
sufficient condition for nonparticipation.

I suspect that most people would reject a policy which
failed to allow for nonparticipation by anyone who wishes

not to participate. One ought not to be *compelled* to assist another in this way. Although we have a duty not to harm another, it is not so clear that anyone has a duty to help others when the help entails the postmortem surrender of a part of the body. Further, since some religious groups (for example, Jehovah's Witnesses and Orthodox Jews) forbid the removal of organs from the body, compelling participation would be a denial of religious freedom. An adequate social policy would not infringe on these basic rights. Hence, any routine salvaging policy must allow for nonparticipation.

If a routine salvaging policy is adopted, hospitals should be required to take cognizance of the objections of religious as well as nonreligious groups opposed to transplantation so that, for anyone who belonged to such a group, salvaging of organs would not be routine. Thus if a patient states that he is, for example, a "Jehovah's Witness" or a member of the "Society for Burial of Intact Bodies," it would be understoood that he is a nonparticipant. Such considerations for nonparticipation would sufficiently safeguard the rights of self-determinism and religious freedom. A policy ought to make it possible for one to exercise his freedom. But it is not necessary to remove all need for effort or initiative in exercising these rights. An appropriate analogy is the selective service system with its provisions for conscientious objection.

Ramsey expresses his concern for the individual having to face the "whole edifice of a hospital practice" if routine salvaging were the operational policy. But this is as much a problem for an effective "giving" policy. To meet the important need for organs to any adequate degree, we would need a more aggressive "giving" policy than we now have. That is, we would need a system of "giving" in which it was expected that most or many would give, or in which hospital officials approached next-of-kin in almost every suitable case to request a donation. Such a policy, no less than one of "taking," would be open to Ramsey's objection. In either case, when a clear prior statement has been

made by the donor the issue of the individual standing up
to the "whole edifice of a hospital practice" does not arise.
When the wishes of the donor are not clear, the potential
for conflict between next-of-kin and hospital is equally
strong in both "taking" and "giving" policies.

A "giving" policy has the disadvantage of requiring
family approval at the time of death. The family in its
most intense moment of grief must sign or refuse to sign
approval forms. Any policy that places the onus of approval on the family at the moment of death is not only
insensitive but doomed to failure. When a young person
(to take as an example a prime candidate for organ transplantation) suddenly and unexpectedly dies, his family
may be dumbfounded, may find it difficult if not impossible to believe that he has died, and yet at the same time
be agonizingly aware of the fact that he has died. In addition to being stunned, a family member in grief often
bears a sense of guilt. When the family is in such a frame
of mind, it would be inclined to see the granting of permission for the removal of any organ from the deceased as
hurting or violating or demeaning the loved one.

When we find ourselves in these "boundary situations"
—when our lives have become unraveled—we need ritual,
routine, and automatic procedures. The procedures ought
to be those that reflect our collective judgment expressed
in more normal times. (The Gallup Poll referred to earlier
is a measure of such a judgment.)

These considerations meet Ramsey's first objection and
provide some support for a routine salvaging policy as
opposed to policies that rely on consent of next-of-kin at
the time of death of the donor.

Ramsey's second major objection to a policy of routine
salvaging is that it "would deprive individuals of the
exercise of the virtue of generosity." It is certainly true
that a routine salvaging policy does not allow for the
exercise of generosity with regard to the particular organs
routinely salvaged. However, there are other avenues open
to anyone for expressing the virtue of generosity.

Of course, as Ramsey says, a society in which "giving and receiving is the rule" will be a better society than one in which good is accomplished only by enforcing policies of "taking." The problem is that experience has demonstrated that the sentiment of benevolence or generosity is not strong enough in a sufficient number of people to operate a society without recourse to rules, regulations, and laws. Hence, this objection reduces to the obvious truth that society would be better if only we all loved one another.

However, social policies must be designed for the society as it is. Is it responsible to allow some to die on the outside chance that someone will be touched by the spirit of generosity? Is it reasonable to allow those who could be saved to die in order to preserve one of many possible avenues for the expression of generosity? Surely, we would need firmer grounds than this to reject policies of "taking."

Robert Veatch argues that routine salvaging proposals entail that body parts are seen "as essentially property of the state to be taken by eminent domain." He maintains that this is a dangerous precedent. One must always be on guard in protecting the individual from the encroachment of the state. However, as social contract theorists have made clear, not all power vested in the state (the collectivity) is a threat to the individual. The more fundamental question we must ask is whether it is in our self-interest to grant the state the right to lay claim to suitable cadaver organs in all cases in which the individual or his family has not expressly denied the state this right.

This question can be answered by considering what sort of "health insurance" one would choose. What would a rational person be willing to pay (or relinquish) in order to have a chance of relief available (through transplantation) in the event of (say) kidney failure? If it is the case (as it appears to be) that the only way a sufficient number of cadaver kidneys can be made available to all persons in need of them is by adopting some policy of routine salvaging, wouldn't the rational person (setting

aside those with religious constraints) be willing to relinquish his right to be buried with his kidneys (should he
die and his kidneys are suitable for transplantation) in
order to have the protection that the availability of cadaver kidneys provides should he suffer kidney failure?
We must ask what a rational person would be willing to
pay in order to have the protection the availability of
cadaver organs provides. The answer is clear. With regard
to organs such as kidneys—given the relatively good chances
of successful transplantation—we (pragmatically) ought to
be (hence, if acting rationally would be) willing to relinquish our right to be buried intact. Organs which, when
transplanted, offer good prospects for relief from a debilitating condition or prevent imminent death, shall be
called "life-saving" organs. The case for routine salvaging
is being made with regard to the limited class of life-
saving organs.

A case for routine salvaging of organs which have not
been very successfully transplanted cannot be made on
this basis. The potential for saving or prolonging the life
of anyone in the "donor" pool should such a person happen to suffer organ failure is extremely small for liver or
lung transplants. Such cadaver organs made available now
would be a contribution to research which may save lives
later (perhaps the next generation). In these sorts of
cases in which immediate benefit to the individual is
extremely remote, the organs (if they are to be obtained
at all) should accordingly be obtained by volunteers. It is
not in the individual's self-interest to vest power in the
state for removal of such organs that would not save or
enhance lives. In this area of social policy, a routine practice ought not to be adopted when it cannot be shown to
conform to consistent or universal enlightened self-interest.
The experimental procedures which require cadaver organs would thus remain as cases for the voluntary exercise
of altruism.

It should be noted that unless there is an incredible,
unanticipated breakthrough in transplantation technique,

only a small percentage of people who die would become actual donors. Hence, it is highly unlikely that a routine salvaging policy would result in our society viewing the body's organs as spare parts, and in that way diminish our respect for the body as an integral part of the person. Because of the unobtrusive way in which a routine salvaging policy can be carried out, it would be less likely to lead to a "spare parts mentality" than an efficient "giving" policy, which would require donor cards or traumatic deathbed decisions.

The most adequate policy will be the one that most completely satisfies the following moral restraints and promotes the following social goals:

(1) Provision of a fitting removal of the body from society.
(2) Protection of the integrity of the corpse.
(3) Protection of the bodily integrity and autonomy of the living.
(4) Saving of lives.
(5) Lack of interference with the attainments of other social objectives.
(6) Assistance for the bereaved survivors.

The following policy of limited routine salvaging optimally meets the criteria of adequacy outlined above:

(1a) Removal of life-saving organs which can be removed without visible damage to the cadaver is routine practice.
(1b) Any individual over eighteen may give all or part of his body for educational, research, therapeutic, or transplantation purposes.
(2) Removal of organs is performed under conditions that do not burden the bereaved persons with the problem.
(3) Permission from the next-of-kin is not required either for removal of life-saving organs or any other uses of the body specified in (1b) for which

the individual gave express permission before death. However, the next-of-kin have the right to object to any of these procedures in which case their objection is controlling.

(4) An individual may object during life to removal of his organs after death, which objection is controlling. The burden of action for making this objection known lies with the individual and/or his next-of-kin. Such objection may be made any time before the organs are removed.

(5) The bequest of any individual who wishes to give all or part of his body for purposes stated in (1b) can be authorized by a card carried by the individual or by written or recorded oral communication from a relative.

V. GENETIC ENGINEERING: PRESENT HAZARDS, FUTURE GAINS

EDITOR'S INTRODUCTION

Among all the recent bio-words generated by the new biology, probably the one most often encountered, apart from *bioethics* itself, is *biohazard*. And nowhere is *biohazard* worked harder than in an area generally known, at least in lay circles, as genetic engineering.

The perils in this line of work have sparked heated controversy—what might be called the Great DNA Debate. Judged on an everyday level and as part of the national picture, the debate has actually been small-scale and on a plane that has been largely intellectual. But its significance, at least, is great. This highly charged discussion has pitted public against scientists (a small segment of the public, at any rate) and even scientists against scientists, a match-up not necessarily contrary to the public interest. The federal government, through agencies representing all concerned groups, has been the referee.

DNA is the symbol for deoxyribonucleic acid, the double-stranded molecule in the cell nucleus that is the bearer of hereditary traits from generation to generation. A number of ways of working with it have been developed in the 1970s. One technique employs the artificial creation of a complete gene, using part of the DNA of a particular species, which is then implanted in a bacterial cell. A second set of complementary techniques, known as recombinant DNA, combines portions of DNA molecules from different species. Such genetic manipulation permits scientists to go beyond hereditary boundaries—boundaries that might never be crossed in the course of natural evolution. Genes of human beings, animals, and plants can be cultivated in bacteria to create new forms of life.

As the selections that follow make clear, there are very good reasons, in the form of potential benefits to human life, for pursuing this research. There are also very good reasons for pursuing it with extreme care. Without such care, some of the new forms of life might well turn out to be antihuman. The problem is one of weighing the advantages against the hazards while keeping the referee (the federal overseer) watchful. Unfortunately, the issues are not only conflicting but very difficult for the nonscientist citizen to grasp. Most people have little difficulty in weighing such matters as death with dignity or abortion or organ transplants; even "test-tube" babies have left the pages of science fiction. As an area of general interest, however, genetic engineering remains the province of a relative handful.

From the outset, many of the scientists directly in the field have been aware of the potential for disaster. A set of national guidelines for research was established in 1976. Though the concerned citizenry has not been a large group, it has been vocal, and its fears have been fed in part by a considerable body of writing, on a popular level, that has had more in common with science fiction than with science itself. For many there is something about genetic research that seems inherently frightening and perhaps improper. Visions of hybrid life being created behind locked laboratory doors is one part of the syndrome. Another is the concern about "playing God." There has been speculation about manipulating genetic endowment in ways that might serve a totalitarian state; even the more optimistic scenarios, in which laboratory-created "good" genes replace "bad," have not been soothing. Researchers label such fears irrational, without scientific base.

The 1976 guidelines still govern the most dangerous categories of experimentation. But in December 1978 the Department of Health, Education and Welfare relaxed the regulations to the extent that about a third of the research work covered by the original guidelines was exempted from control. All such exemptions were in the low-risk categories established in 1976.

The relaxation was in recognition that the worst fears in the field had not been realized. Still, federal regulation remains very real; in some respects, it was broadened by the changes of 1978: provisions were made for bringing private activity under federal supervision. In addition, the National Recombinant DNA Advisory Committee (the supervisory governmental agency) was increased in size from eleven to twenty-five members and broadened to include scientists not directly involved in DNA research and some nonscientists.

The first excerpt in this section, from *Editorial Research Reports,* traces the rise of concern among scientists and lay citizens. There follows, from *U.S. News & World Report,* a survey of the entire DNA field: its nature, scope, potential for benefit, and ever-present hazards.

The third article is by Stanley N. Cohen, a nationally known geneticist and professor of medicine at Stanford University, seeking to distinguish between fact and fiction. Dr. Cohen makes a case for DNA research, with strict controls, from the point of view of a concerned scientist who as early as 1973 had called attention to the real hazards involved.

Sociologist Max Heirich closes the section, and the book, with an assessment of the unresolved issues in the DNA dispute, specifically, and in the pace and direction of scientific inquiry in general.

CONCERNED SCIENTISTS AND A CONCERNED CITIZENRY [1]

The study of genetics has come a long way since Gregor Mendel's experiments with pea plants demonstrated the

---

[1] From pamphlet entitled "Genetic Research," by Sandra Stencel, staff writer. *Editorial Research Reports.* v 1, no 12, p 234-43. Mr. 25, '77. Reprinted by permission.

fundamental laws of inheritance. Mendel, a 19th-century Austrian monk, showed that for each physical trait, every individual possessed two "factors," or what later came to be known as genes. Biologists had only fragmentary knowledge of the genetic process until the mid-20th century. It was known that genes were arranged in linear sequence along chromosomes, which are present in the nucleus of every living cell, but nothing was known about the molecular structure of genetic material.

In 1944, however, three biochemists at the Rockefeller Institute—Oswald T. Avery, Colin MacCloud and Maclyn McCarty—learned that genes were composed of deoxyribonucleic acid (DNA). The next step was to determine the structure of the complex DNA molecule. This was accomplished in England in 1953 by two Cambridge scientists, Francis H. C. Crick and Maurice H. F. Wilkins, and an American colleague, James D. Watson. . . .

Recombinant DNA, or gene-splicing, was made possible by a series of independent discoveries in the past 15 years. In 1962 scientists discovered that bacterial cells contain a substance, called a restriction enzyme, that acts as a chemical scalpel to split DNA molecules into specific segments. Ten years later the enzyme was purified from bacteria by microbiologist Herbert W. Boyer and his colleagues at the University of California at San Francisco. Then two researchers at Stanford—Janet E. Mertz and Ronald W. Davis—discovered that the split DNA fragments had sticky ends that enabled them to be joined together with other DNA fragments. Putting these discoveries together, Dr. Stanley N. Cohen of Stanford University School of Medicine [author of article that follows] and his assistant, Annie C. Y. Chang, were able to construct in a test tube a biologically functional DNA molecule that combined genetic information from two different sources—in this case, two different plasmids found in E. Coli bacteria [Escherichia coli, commonly found in human intestines].

Subsequent experiments by Cohen and Chang, in collaboration with Herbert W. Boyer and Robert B. Hellig of the University of California at San Francisco, showed that genes from another species of bacterium, Staphylococcus aureus, could be transplanted into E. Coli. Further experimentation demonstrated that animal DNA—specifically, ribosomal DNA from the South African toad—could be linked with plasmid DNA to form recombinant molecules that would reproduce in E. Coli. A proliferation of recombinant DNA work followed, resulting in the insertion into bacteria of animal DNA from fruit flies, toads, mice, sea urchins, slime molds and chickens.

Organized Effort to Assess Research Risks

Cohen and his colleagues recognized from the beginning that the construction of some kinds of novel gene combinations might have a potential for biological hazard. At first the primary concern was that certain gene-splicing experiments might increase the risks of work with cancer viruses. One of the first scientists to voice this concern publicly was Paul Berg of Stanford, who decided to abandon plans to introduce genes from a tumor virus into E. Coli bacteria after his colleagues suggested that the resulting organism might spread cancer to humans.

Berg helped to organize a conference in New Hampshire in July 1973 to review the available information on recombinant research and to assess the potential risks. Those attending the conference—the Gordon Research Conference on Nucleic Acids—sent an open letter to Dr. Philip Handler, president of the National Academy of Sciences, warning that new organisms "with biological activity of an unpredictable nature" could be created by these experiments. They urged him to "establish a study committee to consider this problem and to recommend specific actions or guidelines should that seem appropriate."

A committee was formed, with Paul Berg as chairman, and in a now-famous letter to *Science* magazine in July 1974 [p. 303], it recommended that certain types of recombinant DNA research be voluntarily deferred "until the potential hazards . . . have been better evaluated or until adequate methods are developed for preventing their spread. . . ." The types of research covered by the moratorium were (1) formation of bacteria resistant to antibiotics, (2) linkage of DNA molecules with tumor-causing viruses, and (3) introduction of toxin-formation or antibiotic-resistance genes into bacteria that did not naturally contain such genes. Berg's committee also asked the director of the National Institutes of Health [NIH], Robert S. Stone, to set up an advisory committee to evaluate potential hazards in this research, devise safety procedures and develop guidelines for researchers working with potentially hazardous DNA molecules. Finally, the Berg committee said that an international conference should be convened as soon as possible.

The Berg committee's call for a voluntary moratorium was called an unprecedented event. In fact, the American Chemical Society listed it among the most important scientific events of the last 100 years. The moratorium was widely reported by the press and produced an international reaction. Stone quickly announced his intention to establish an advisory committee, as recommended, and he offered financial support for an international meeting. In England, the Advisory Board for the Research Councils, the prime source of government funding for civil research in Britain, set up a committee to assess the potential hazards and benefits of genetic engineering. In the interim, the board asked all of its units to suspend any experiments cited by the Berg committee as particularly dangerous.

In his presidential address to the British Association for the Advancement of Science in September 1974, molecular biologist Sir John Kendrew commended the Berg committee's actions and suggested the establishment of a permanent international monitoring body of molecular biologists who would assess gene-transfer experiments. On the other hand, the influential British journal *Nature,* in an editorial on September 6, 1974, rejected a suggestion that it cease publication of articles on research covered by the proposed moratorium. In October 1974, DNA recombination came under discussion at a Pugwash Conference in Austria and at an international symposium in Davos, Switzerland. Most participants at the Davos conference acknowledged the "enormous dangers" posed by recombination, but they concluded that controls would be "impractical and unenforceable."

Recommendations From 1975 Conference

The international meeting proposed by the Berg committee was held in February 1975 at the Asilomar Conference Center in Pacific Grove, Calif. It was sponsored by the National Academy of Sciences and was supported by the National Institutes of Health and the National Science Foundation; 150 persons from 16 countries attended. They revealed a wide divergence of opinion in the scientific community. Nobel laureate Joshua Lederberg of Stanford expressed his dismay at the prospect that guidelines might end up "crystallized into legislation." James D. Watson of Harvard said that guidelines would be essentially unenforceable, and that therefore the best tactic was to rely on the common sense of those doing the research. Some participants argued that the risks were too remote to justify limiting the freedom of scientific inquiry. Others insisted that the moral responsibility to protect the public was more important than academic freedom or individual success.

In the end, the participants concluded that "most of the work . . . should proceed." They ranked the experiments by potential risk and specified safety precautions for each level. And they favored a ban on experiments that, while feasible, "present such serious dangers that their performance should not be undertaken at this time."

Nicholas Wade of *Science* magazine described the actions taken at Asilomar as "a rare, if not unique, example of safety precautions being imposed on a technical development before, instead of after, the first occurrence of the hazard being guarded against." Jack McWethy of *U.S. News & World Report* called the conference a landmark "because it provided for all scientists a working illustration of how specialists can examine and, when necessary, limit their research for the public good long before the issues are dragged into the . . . political arena."

Immediately after the conference, the NIH Advisory Committee on Recombinant DNA, which had been set up in October 1974, held its first meeting in San Francisco to begin translating the mandate of Asilomar into firm guidelines binding on all researchers receiving NIH grants. At a second meeting, held May 12-13, 1975, in Bethesda, Md., a subcommittee under the chairmanship of Dr. David Hogness was appointed to draft the guidelines. The first draft, made public the following July 18-19 at a meeting in Woods Hole, Mass., was widely criticized as being weaker than the rules agreed upon at Asilomar. Two Boston-centered groups, Science for the People and the Boston Area Recombinant DNA Group, organized a petition drive against the draft guidelines. Eventually a new NIH subcommittee was appointed to revise them.

The draft guidelines finally adopted by the NIH advisory committee at La Jolla, Calif., on December 5, 1975, were, according to Nicholas Wade, "demonstratively stricter than the Asilomar guidelines. . . ." Although the guidelines were criticized in some quarters, they were approved by the National Institutes of Health and released on June 23, 1976.

During the months of debate that preceded the issuing of the guidelines, questions were raised about the possibility that organisms containing recombinant DNA molecules might escape and harm the environment. The National Institutes of Health pointed out that the guidelines prohibit the deliberate release of such organisms. Nevertheless it agreed to review the possible environmental impact of genetic experiments. A draft of the environmental impact statement was released for public comment on August 26, 1976.

Emergence of Citizen Oversight

Science today is facing the equivalent of the Protestant Reformation, according to University of Chicago philosopher Stephen Toulmin. Likening the scientific establishment to the 16th century church, Toulmin said that the people are tired of being shut out of science's "ecclesiastical courts" and are demanding to be let in. The scientist "priest," he predicted, is going to be overthrown.

In the past, the public tended to acquiesce in the judgment of scientists in the assumption that any advance of knowledge was necessarily beneficial. But in recent years, trust and approval have given way to suspicion and apprehension among increasing numbers of Americans. Behind the public's misgivings is a litany of known or suspected hazards that were the product of scientific research: DDT, cyclamates, asbestos, PSB, vinyl chloride, radioactivity, aerosol propellants, food additives, Kepone.

The upshot of all this appears to be that "the American public is coming to regard scientific research with what might be termed a *Code Napoleon* attitude," according to George Alexander, science writer for the Los Angeles *Times.* "Just as that French legal system presumes that an individual is guilty of an alleged crime and places the burden of [proof of] innocence upon the accused, so does this evolving public attitude presuppose that new research is more likely to be harmful than beneficial, that disadvantages are more likely to outweigh advantages.

Nowhere is this public attitude more evident today than in the debate over the safety of recombinant DNA research. In barely five years, it already has given rise to Vietnam-type protest groups and to city council and state legislative hearings from Cambridge, Mass., to Sacramento, Calif. . . .

The first local rumblings of discontent came in Ann Arbor, Mich. Early in 1975, the regents of the University of Michigan began to consider a plan to upgrade some laboratories to the P3 level of containment [third on a scale of 1-4]. This set off a debate which went on for over a year. At several public hearings the plan was opposed by the Ann Arbor Ecology Center and a few faculty members, notably Shaw Livermore, a professor of American history, and Susan Wright, associate professor of humanities. Depite the opposition, the regents in May 1976 voted 6 to 1 to proceed with the research.

Community Action on Recombinant Research

The debate in Ann Arbor was largely confined to the university. A much broader public debate took place in Cambridge, Mass. The controversy over recombinant DNA erupted in June 1976 after a weekly newspaper, the Boston *Phoenix,* reported Harvard's plan to convert an existing laboratory into a P3 facility. Some faculty members, led by Nobel laureate George Wald and his wife, Harvard biologist Ruth Hubbard, expressed their opposition to Cambridge Mayor Alfred E. Vellucci. He called a public meeting on the matter, saying "We want to be damned sure the people of Cambridge won't be affected by anything that would crawl out of that laboratory."

The Cambridge City Council considered the issue on June 23 at a hearing attended by nearly 500 persons and again on July 7. At the second meeting the council imposed a three-month moratorium on moderate and high-risk DNA experiments until a citizens' review board could study the problem. This was considered a precedent-setting action for involving the public in decision-making regarding biological research.

The nine members of the Cambridge Experimentation Review Board met twice a week for five months (the moratorium was extended) and issued a report in January 1977 declaring that "knowledge, whether for its own sake or for its potential benefits to mankind, cannot serve as a justification for introducing risks to the public unless an informed citizenry is willing to accept those risks." The review board decided unanimously that it was prepared to accept those risks, and it recommended that the research be allowed to continue.

However, in the belief that "a predominantly lay citizen group can face a technical scientific matter of general and deep public concern, educate itself appropriately to the task, and reach a fair decision," the panel concluded that the safety guidelines developed by the National Institutes of Health did not go far enough. The board recommended some additional measures, including the preparation of a safety manual, training of personnel to minimize accidents, and inclusion of a community representative on the NIH-mandated "biohazards committees" at Harvard and the Massachusetts Institute of Technology. The review board also recommended that the city set up a permanent citizen biohazards committee to monitor the research at the universities and report violations.

On February 7, 1977, the Cambridge City Council endorsed the board's recommendations after rejecting a proposal by Mayor Vellucci to ban the research altogether. "What happened in Cambridge is of major national importance," said Stanley Jones, a staff member of the Senate Health Subcommittee. "It is the first time a public community group has looked at an issue in science and made recommendations on what it thought was appropriate."

The year-long debate in Cambridge spurred action in other communities. In San Diego, Calif., the city's Quality of Life Board acted at the request of Mayor Pete Wilson to set up a committee to review DNA work at the University of California at San Diego. After hearing an array of witnesses, the committee in February 1977 submitted a report generally endorsing the NIH guidelines. But in addition, it recommended that (1) the city council consider the desirability of confining all gene-splicing research to P3 laboratories, (2) the university refrain from experiments requiring P4 facilities, (3) it notify the city of any P3 experiment requiring the highest degree of biological containment, and (4) an ordinance be passed to bring industry and private researchers within the control of the guidelines.

In Madison, Wis., the city council recently appointed a committee to study the possible hazards of recombinant DNA research at the University of Wisconsin. A citizen review board also was set up recently in Princeton, N.J. Public hearings on the question have been held in several other university towns, including Bloomington, Ind. (Indiana University), New Haven, Conn. (Yale), and Palo Alto, Calif. (Stanford). . . .

Significance of Public Participation in Science

The calls to prohibit or slow down the research seem threatening and irrational to many of those scientists who first pointed to the risks. The public's response might make scientists reluctant to question the consequences of any future research for fear of generating "unjustified fears" and "opening themselves up to attack," according to Professor Mark Ptashne of Harvard. . . .

So far, the scientist's fear of citizen review seems unjustified. Most public bodies that have considered the recombinant DNA controversy have endorsed the guidelines issued by the National Institutes of Health with minor changes. The report submitted by the Cambridge Experimentation Review Board was praised by both critics and supporters of recombination. "It proved that even complex scientific issues can be understood by lay people who devote the necessary time and energy to the problem," wrote Dr. David Baltimore of the Massachusetts Institute of Technology. As science increases its powers to modify all aspects of society, more and more people are taking the time to question the implications of scientific research.

CREATING NEW FORMS OF LIFE— BLESSING OR CURSE? [2]

Reprinted from "U.S. News & World Report"

A wave of excitement—mingled with growing anxiety— is spreading through the nation as major laboratories rush into something that is called "genetic engineering."

Experiments already are making breakthroughs into a whole new dimension in science: the creation of new forms of life.

The process takes the gene for a specific characteristic out of one organism and transplants it into another to produce a desired change.

That technique holds the hope of curing certain genetic diseases by replacing defective genes with healthy ones.

It has the potential to produce new drugs, "super-strains" of wheat, and bizarre but useful animals—bypass-ing the millions of years required by the evolutionary process in nature.

Possible Risk

There is another side to this great breakthrough, however:

If these experiments were somehow to go awry and deadly organisms escaped from the laboratory, they could irreversibly cripple life on earth. . . .

Altogether, more than 80 university laboratories in the U.S. are working with these so-called recombinant-DNA techniques along with at least nine private companies.

Their controversial research centers on deoxyribonu-cleic acid, DNA, the complex molecule that transmits heredity in all forms of life on earth.

The recombinant-DNA technique, emerging in the early 1970s, allows scientists for the first time to identify a characteristic from the DNA molecule of one species

[2] Article in *U.S. News & World Report.* v 82, no 14, p 80-1. Ap. 11, '77. Copyright 1977 U.S. News & World Report, Inc.

and to transplant it into another. This literally permits them to "recombine" genetic characteristics into hybrid forms of life unique in nature.

Among higher animals, this might mean giving a cat a bark, an alligator fur or a dog hooves instead of paws. These illustrations are considered farfetched at present, but work is under way on parallel experiments with lower forms of life—bacteria and viruses—to alter their characteristics in ways that nature never intended.

Not since the public began to debate the potential good and evil of nuclear power has any scientific issue touched off such a controversy as gene engineering has caused.

Many citizens, along with a significant number of scientists, fear that experimenters may accidentally create a biological monster while in search of the alluring benefits they foresee.

Paul Berg, a pioneer in the field at his Stanford University biochemistry laboratory, says the most important practical benefit from recombinant-DNA research will be new knowledge about human genes and chromosomes. This, he says, "will make the diagnosis, prevention and cure of disease more rational and effective."

However, Ethan Signer, a biologist at the Massachusetts Institute of Technology, argues that there are safer ways to obtain the same kind of research information. Says Singer: "It's risky, maybe even incredibly risky to us, to the biosphere, to the future. We're going to tinker with the human-gene pool, and we don't need it." . . .

Many involved in genetic engineering say the real question is: At what speed should it be allowed to progress and at what risk to the public?

As they see it, the research has already moved beyond the point where it could just be stopped. Laboratories all over the world are working with recombinant-DNA techniques. The research and the risks would be continued even if the experiments were banned in the U.S.

To avoid the kind of biological nightmares conjured

by critics, safety engineers see two approaches in protecting the public—other than simply avoiding a particular experiment.

One is to provide top-quality physical containment. This means special laboratories to protect the scientists and allow no air or contaminated materials to leave the building without being sterilized. There are four degrees of physical containment and, at the moment, there is not a laboratory in the country approved for the most dangerous kinds of experiments.

The second approach is biological containment—specially designed bacteria and viruses that are used as guinea pigs and made so that they cannot survive outside the laboratory's protective environment. One strain, for example, will die if it comes into contact with salts commonly found in the human body and in sewers.

Despite such precautions, some scientists warn, it is possible that experimentally altered bacteria or viruses will escape. There are breakdowns in equipment and, most commonly, human failures.

Stephen Toulmin of the University of Chicago explains that once there is an accidental release, a new kind of environmental contaminant is created. Instead of being diluted with passage of time, as is the case with a toxic chemical spill, says Toulmin, "any 'rogue' agents produced artificially in the course of the research will have the power to multiply themselves and spread throughout the population at large."

Another concern to many is the type of bacteria that scientists have chosen as their prime guinea pig. It is called E. coli, and different strains of it are commonly found in nearly all mammals, including humans. Biologists use it because they know more about its genetic makeup than almost any other form of life.

A Ready Home

If an altered E. coli did escape physical containment, it would find a ready home in the intestines of the humans who work in the lab. They, in turn, would unknowingly carry the mutated E. coli out of the lab in their bodies.

Visions of drug-resistant bacteria, spreading contagious, uncontrollable diseases across the land, are among the wildest scenarios associated with recombinant-DNA research. Few scientists deny that they are possible, but most regard the possibility as extremely remote—comparable to the chances that a meteorite will strike New York City and kill a million people.

The critics themselves are intrigued by the possibilities for using this revolutionary tool to unlock secrets of genetic structure in all forms of life.

Food production may become a major beneficiary of recombinant-DNA techniques. A potential example:

Such crops as corn require huge amounts of nitrogen fertilizers. Soybeans, on the other hand, need almost none of these fertilizers because they provide a home in their roots for a bacterium called rhizobium, which gathers nitrogen from the air and "fixes" it in the soil for later use by the soybean.

Now scientists are exploring the possibility of designing a bacterium that could live amiably in corn or wheat, fixing nitrogen as a fertilizer for that plant. In fact, British researchers have already created the world's first nitrogen-fixing E. coli bacterium, though it is not yet capable of surviving outside the laboratory.

The use of recombinant-DNA techniques on humans may be just five years away. In genetic diseases that affect the blood, for instance, gene engineers could draw from the bone marrow some of the defective cells that should be making blood, then add to them the genetic subunits they lack to function properly.

Says David Baltimore, Nobel Prize-winning cancer researcher: "It could be fast, painless and inexpensive. I have no doubt that in five to 10 years this kind of experiment will be attempted."

With the scientists themselves unable to agree on the magnitude of possible risks and benefits in recombinant-

DNA research, public bodies have thus far opted for a go-slow approach. As one instance, the city council of Cambridge, Mass., is allowing research to continue there, but only under tougher guidelines than those published by NIH.

No End to Debate

Action to control the scope of DNA experiments locally is also being considered in the New York and California legislatures. For the most part, citizen and university committees across the nation are allowing the low-risk experiments and banning those that require the most elaborate kinds of physical containment. Nonetheless, public debate about continuing even the most rudimentary experiments involving recombinant DNA is almost certain to continue.

"We will not go gentle into the new order of the world that is being offered here," said Ted Howard of the People's Business Commission at a recent DNA conference in Washington, D.C. The theme song of those protesting at the National Academy of Science meeting: "We shall not be cloned."

RECOMBINANT DNA: FACT AND FICTION [3]

Almost three years ago, I joined with a group of scientific colleagues in publicly calling attention to possible biohazards of certain kinds of experiments that could be carried out with newly developed techniques for the propagation of genes from diverse sources in bacteria. Because of the newness and relative simplicity of these techniques, we were concerned that experiments involving certain genetic combinations that seemed to us to be hazardous might be performed before adequate consideration had

[3] Article by Stanley N. Cohen, molecular geneticist and professor of medicine, Stanford University. *Science.* v 195, no 4279, p 654-7. F. 18, '77. Copyright 1977 by the American Association for the Advancement of Science.

been given to the potential dangers. Contrary to what was believed by many observers, our concerns pertained to a few very specific types of experiments that could be carried out with the new techniques, not to the techniques themselves.

Guidelines have long been available to protect laboratory workers and the general public against known hazards associated with the handling of certain chemicals, radioisotopes, and pathogenic microorganisms; but because of the newness of recombinant DNA techniques, no guidelines were yet available for this research. My colleagues and I wanted to be sure that these new techniques would not be used, for example, for the construction of streptococci or pneumococci resistant to penicillin, or for the creation of *Escherichia coli* capable of synthesizing botulinum toxin or diphtheria toxin. We asked that these experiments not be done, and also called for deferral of construction of bacterial recombinants containing tumor virus genes until the implications of such experiments could be given further consideration.

During the past two years, much fiction has been written about "recombinant DNA research." What began as an act of responsibility by scientists, including a number of those involved in the development of the new techniques, has become the breeding ground for a horde of publicists—most poorly informed, some well-meaning, some self-serving. In this article I attempt to inject some relevant facts into the extensive public discussion of recombinant DNA research.

Some Basic Information

Recombinant DNA research is not a single entity, but rather it is a group of techniques that can be used for a wide variety of experiments. Much confusion has resulted from a lack of understanding of this point by many who have written about the subject. Recombinant DNA techniques, like chemicals on a shelf, are neither good nor bad per se. Certain experiments that can be done with these techniques are likely to be hazardous (just as certain experiments done with combinations of chemicals taken from the shelf will be hazardous), and there is universal agreement that such recombinant DNA experiments should not be done. Other experiments in which the very same techniques are used—such as taking apart a DNA molecule and putting segments of it back together again—are without conceivable hazard, and anyone who has looked into the matter has concluded that these experiments can be done without concern.

Then, there is the area "in between." For many experiments, there is no evidence of biohazard, but there is also no certainty that there is not a hazard. For these experiments, guidelines have been developed in an attempt to match a level of containment with a degree of hypothetical risk. Perhaps the single point that has been most misunderstood in the controversy about recombinant DNA research, is that discussion of "risk" in the middle category of experiments relates entirely to hypothetical and speculative possibilities, not expected consequences or even phenomena that seem likely to occur on the basis of what is known. Unfortunately, much of the speculation has been interpreted as fact.

There is nothing novel about the principle of matching a level of containment with the level of anticipated hazard; the containment procedures used for pathogenic bacteria, toxic substances, and radioisotopes attempt to do this. However, the containment measures used in these areas address themselves only to known hazards and do not attempt to protect against the unknown. If the same principle of protecting only against known or expected hazards were followed in recombinant DNA research, there would be no containment whatsoever except for a very few experiments. In this instance, we are asking not only that there be no evidence of hazard, but that there be positive evidence that there is no hazard. In developing guidelines for recombinant DNA research, we have attempted to take precautionary steps to protect ourselves against hazards that are not known to exist—and this unprecedented act of caution is so novel that it has been widely misinterpreted as implying the imminence or at least the likelihood of danger.

Much has been made of the fact that, even if a particular recombinant DNA molecule shows no evidence of being hazardous at the present time, we are unable to say for certain that it will not devastate our planet some years hence. Of course this view is correct; similarly, we are unable to say for certain that the vaccines we are administering to millions of children do not contain agents that will produce contagious cancer some years hence, we are unable to say for certain that a virulent virus will not be brought to the United States next winter by a traveler from abroad, causing a nationwide fatal epidemic of a hitherto unknown disease—and we are unable to say for certain that novel hybrid plants being bred around the world will not suddenly become weeds that will overcome our major food crops and cause worldwide famine.

The statement that potential hazards could result from certain experiments involving recombinant DNA techniques is akin to the statement that a vaccine injected today into millions of people *could* lead to infectious cancer in 20 years, a pandemic caused by a traveler-borne virus *could* devastate the United States, or a new plant species *could* uncontrollably destroy the world's food supply. We have no reason to expect that any of these things will happen, but we are unable to say for certain that they will not happen. Similarly, we are unable to guarantee that any of man's efforts to influence the earth's weather, explore space, modify crops, or cure disease will not carry with them the seeds for the ultimate destruction of civilization. Can we in fact point to one major area of human activity where one can say *for certain* that there is zero risk? Potentially, we could respond to such risks by taking measures such as prohibiting foreign travel to reduce the hazard of deadly virus importation and stopping experimentation with hybrid plants. It is possible to develop plausible "scare scenarios" involving virtually any activity or process, and these would have as much (or as little) basis in fact as most of the scenarios involving recombinant DNA. But we must distinguish fear of the unknown from fear that has some basis in fact; this appears to be the crux of the controversy surrounding recombinant DNA.

Unfortunately, the public has been led to believe that the biohazards described in various scenarios are likely or probable outcomes of recombinant DNA research. "If the scientists themselves are concerned enough to raise the issue," goes the fiction, "the problem is probably much worse than anyone will admit." However, the simple fact is that there is no evidence that a bacterium carrying any recombinant DNA molecule poses a hazard beyond the hazard that can be anticipated from the known properties of the components of the recombinant. And experiments involving genes that produce toxic substances or pose other known hazards are prohibited.

Freedom of Scientific Inquiry

This issue has been raised repeatedly during discussions of recombinant DNA research. "The time has come," the critics charge, "for scientists to abandon their long-held belief that they should be free to pursue the acquisition of new knowledge regardless of the consequences." The fact is that no one has proposed that freedom of inquiry should extend to scientific experiments that endanger public safety. Yet, "freedom of scientific inquiry" is repeatedly raised as a straw-man issue by critics who imply that somewhere there are those who argue that there should be no restraint whatsoever on research.

Instead, the history of this issue is one of self-imposed restraint by scientists from the very start. The scientific group that first raised the question of possible hazard in some kinds of recombinant DNA experiments included most of the scientists involved in the development of the techniques—and their concern was made public so that other investigators who might not have adequately considered the possibility of hazard could exercise appropriate restraint. While most scientists would defend their right to freedom of scientific thought and discourse, I do not know of anyone who has proposed that scientists should be free to do whatever experiments they choose regardless of the consequences.

Interference with "Evolutionary Wisdom"

Some critics of recombinant DNA research ask us to believe that the process of evolution of plants, animals, and microbes has remained delicately controlled for millions of years, and that the construction of recombinant DNA molecules now threatens the master plan of evolution. Such thinking, which requires a belief that nature is endowed with wisdom, intent, and foresight, is alien to most post-Darwinian biologists. Moreover, there is no evidence that the evolutionary process is delicately controlled by nature. To the contrary, man has long ago modified the process of evolution, and biological evolution continues to be influenced by man. Primitive man's domestication of animals and cultivation of crops provided an "unnatural" advantage to certain biological species and a consequent perturbation of evolution. The later creation by man of hybrid plants and animals has resulted in the propagation of new genetic combinations that are not the products of natural evolution. In the microbiological world, the use of antimicrobial agents to treat bacterial infections and the advent of mass immunization programs against viral disease has made untenable the thesis of delicate evolutionary control.

A recent letter [Chargaff, *Science,* Je. 4, '76] that has been widely quoted by critics of recombinant DNA research asks, "Have we the right to counteract irreversibly the evolutionary wisdom of millions of years . . . ?" It is this so-called evolutionary wisdom that gave us the gene combinations for bubonic plague, smallpox, yellow fever, typhoid, polio, diabetes, and cancer. It is this wisdom that continues to give us uncontrollable diseases such as Lassa fever, Marburg virus, and very recently the Marburg-related hemorrhagic fever virus, which has resulted in nearly 100 percent mortality in infected individuals in Zaire and the Sudan. The acquisition and use of all biological and medical knowledge constitutes an intentional and continuing assault on evolutionary wisdom. Is this the "warfare against nature" that some critics fear from recombinant DNA?

How About the Benefits?

For all but a very few experiments, the risks of recombinant DNA research are speculative. Are the benefits equally speculative or is there some factual basis for expecting that benefits will occur from this technique? I believe that the anticipation of benefits has a substantial basis in fact, and that the benefits fall into two principal categories: (i) advancement of fundamental scientific and medical knowledge, and (ii) possible practical applications.

In the short space of $3\frac{1}{2}$ years, the use of the recombinant DNA technology has already been of major importance in the advancement of fundamental knowledge. We need to understand the structure and function of genes, and this methodology provides a way to isolate large quantities of specific segments of DNA in pure form. For example, recombinant DNA methodology has provided us with much information about the structure of plasmids that cause antibiotic resistance in bacteria, and has given us insights into how these elements propagate themselves, how they evolve, and how their genes are regulated. In the past, our inability to isolate specific genetic regions of the chromosomes of higher organisms has limited our understanding of the genes of complex cells. Now use of recombinant DNA techniques has provided knowledge about how genes are organized into chromosomes and how gene expression is controlled. With such knowledge we can begin to learn how defects in the structure of such genes alter their function.

On a more practical level, recombinant DNA techniques potentially permit the construction of bacterial strains that can produce biologically important substances such as antibodies and hormones. Although the full expression of higher organism DNA that is necessary to accomplish such production has not yet been achieved in bacteria, the steps that need to be taken to reach this goal are defined, and we can reasonably expect that the introduction of appropriate "start" and "stop" control signals into recombinant DNA molecules will enable the expression of animal cell genes. On an even shorter time scale, we can expect recombinant DNA techniques to revolutionize the product of antibiotics, vitamins, and medically and industrially useful chemicals by eliminating the need to grow and process the often exotic bacterial and fungal strains currently used as sources for such agents. We can anticipate the construction of modified antimicrobial agents that are not destroyed by the antibiotic inactivating enzymes responsible for drug resistance in bacteria.

In the area of vaccine production, we can anticipate the construction of specific bacterial strains able to produce desired antigenic products, eliminating the present need for immunization with killed or attenuated specimens of disease-causing viruses.

One practical application of recombinant DNA technology in the area of vaccine production is already close to being realized. An *E. coli* plasmid coding for an enteric toxin fatal to livestock has been taken apart, and the toxin gene has been separated from the remainder of the plasmid. The next step is to cut away a small segment of the toxin-producing gene so that the substance produced by the resulting gene in *E. coli* will not have toxic properties but will be immunologically active in stimulating antibody production.

Other benefits from recombinant DNA research in the areas of food and energy production are more speculative. However, even in these areas there is a scientific basis for expecting that the benefits will someday be realized. The limited availability of fertilizers and the potential hazards associated with excessive use of nitrogen fertilizers now limits the yields of grain and other crops, but agricultural experts suggests that transplantation of the nitrogenase system from the chromosomes of certain bacteria into plants or into other bacteria that live symbiotically with food crop plants may eliminate the need for fertilizers. For many years, scientists have modified the heredity of plants by comparatively primitive techniques. Now there is a means of doing this with greater precision than has been possible previously.

Certain algae are known to produce hydrogen from water, using sunlight as energy. This process potentially can yield a virtually limitless source of pollution-free energy if technical and biochemical problems indigenous to the known hydrogen-producing organisms can be solved. Recombinant DNA techniques offer a possible means of solution to these problems.

It is ironic that some of the most vocal opposition to recombinant DNA research has come from those most concerned about the environment. The ability to manipulate microbial genes offers the promise of more effective utilization of renewable resources for mankind's food and energy needs; the status quo offers the prospect of progressive and continuing devastation of the environment. Yet, some environmentalists have been misled into taking what I believe to be an antienvironmental position on the issue of recombinant DNA.

The NIH Guidelines

Even if hazards are speculative and the potential benefits are significant and convincing, wouldn't it still be better to carry out recombinant DNA experiments under conditions that provide an added measure of safety—just in case some of the conjectural hazards prove to be real?

This is exactly what is required under the NIH (National Institutes of Health) guidelines for recombinant DNA research:

1) These guidelines prohibit experiments in which there is some scientific basis for anticipating that a hazard will occur. In addition, they prohibit experiments in which a hazard, although it might be entirely speculative, was judged by NIH to be potentially serious enough to warrant prohibition of the experiment. The types of experiment that were the basis of the initial "moratorium" are included in this category; contrary to the statements of some who have written about recombinant DNA research, there has in fact been no lifting of the original restrictions on such experiments.

2) The NIH guidelines require that a large class of other experiments be carried out in P4 (high level) containment facilities of the type designed for work with the most hazardous naturally occurring microorganisms known to man (such as Lassa fever virus, Marburg virus, and Zaire hemorrhagic fever virus). It is difficult to imagine more hazardous self-propagating biological agents than such viruses, some of which lead to nearly 100 percent mortality in infected individuals. The P4 containment requires a specially built laboratory with airlocks and filters, biological safety cabinets, clothing changes for personnel, autoclaves within the facility, and the like. This level of containment is required for recombinant DNA experiments for which there is at present no evidence of hazard, but for which it is perceived that the hazard might be potentially serious if conjectural fears prove to be real. There are at present only four or five installations in the United States where P4 experiments could be carried out.

3) Experiments associated with a still lesser degree of hypothetical risk can be conducted in P3 containment facilities. These are also specially constructed laboratories requiring double door entrances, negative air pressure, and special air filtration devices. Facilities where P3 experiments can be performed are limited in number, but they exist at some universities.

4) Experiments in which the hazard is considered unlikely to be serious even if it occurs still require labora-

tory procedures (P2 containment) that have for years been considered sufficient for research with such pathogenic bacteria as *Salmonella typhosa, Clostridium botulinum,* and *Cholera vibrio.* The NIH guidelines require that P2 facilities be used for work with bacteria carrying interspecies recombinant DNA molecules that have shown no evidence of being hazardous—and even for some recombinant DNA experiments in which there is substantial evidence of lack of hazard.

5) The PI (lowest) level of containment can be used only for recombinant DNA molecules that potentially can be made by ordinary biological gene exchange in bacteria. Conformity to even this lowest level of containment in the laboratory requires decontamination of work surfaces daily and after spills of biological materials, the use of mechanical pipetting devices or cotton plugged pipettes by workers, a pest control program, and decontamination of liquid and solid waste leaving the laboratory.

In other areas of actual or potential biological hazard, physical containment is all that microbiologists have had to rely upon; if the Lassa fever virus were to be released inadvertently from a P4 facility, there would be no further barrier to prevent the propagation of this virus which is known to be deadly and for which no specific therapy exists. However, the NIH guidelines for recombinant DNA research have provided for an additional level of safety for workers and the public: This is a system of biological containment that is designed to reduce by many orders of magnitude the chance of propagation outside the laboratory of microorganisms used as hosts for recombinant DNA molecules.

An inevitable consequence of these containment procedures is that they have made it difficult for the public to appreciate that most of the hazards under discussion are conjectural. Because in the past, governmental agencies have often been slow to respond to clear and definite dangers in other areas of technology, it has been inconceivable to scientists working in other fields and to the public at large that an extensive and costly federal machinery would have been established to provide protection in this area of research unless severe hazards were known to exist. The fact that recombinant DNA research has prompted international meetings, extensive coverage in the news media, and governmental intervention at the federal level has been perceived by the public as prima facie evidence that this research must be more dangerous than all the rest. The scientific community's response has been to establish increasingly elaborate procedures to police itself—but these very acts of scientific caution and responsibility have only served to perpetuate and strengthen the general belief that the hazards under discussion must be clearcut and imminent in order for such steps to be necessary.

It is worth pointing out that despite predictions of imminent disaster from recombinant DNA experiments, the fact remains that during the past $3\frac{1}{2}$ years, many billions of bacteria containing a wide variety of recombinant DNA molecules have been grown and propagated in the United States and abroad, incorporating DNA from viruses, protozoa, insects, sea urchins, frogs, yeast, mammals, and unrelated bacterial species into *E. coli*, without hazardous consequences so far as I am aware. And the majority of these experiments were carried out prior to the strict containment procedures specified in the current federal guidelines.

Despite the experience thus far, it will always be valid to argue that recombinant DNA molecules that seem safe today may prove hazardous tomorrow. One can no more prove the safety of a particular genetic combination under all imaginable circumstances than one can prove that currently administered vaccines do not contain an undetected self-propagating agent capable of producing cancer in the future, or that a hybrid plant created today will not lead to disastrous consequences some years hence. No matter what evidence is collected to document the safety of a new therapeutic agent, a vaccine, a process, or a particular kind of recombinant DNA molecule, one can always conjure up the possibility of future hazards that cannot be disproved. When one deals with conjecture, the number of possible hazards is unlimited; the experiments that can be done to establish the absence of hazard are finite in number.

Those who argue that we should not use recombinant DNA techniques until or unless we are absolutely certain that there is zero risk fail to recognize that no one will ever be able to guarantee total freedom from risk in any significant human activity. All that we can reasonably expect is a mechanism for dealing responsibly with hazards that are known to exist or which appear likely on the basis of information that is known. Beyond this, we can and should exercise caution in any activity that carries us into previously uncharted territory, whether it is recombinant DNA research, creation of a new drug or vaccine, or bringing a spaceship back to Earth from the moon.

Today, as in the past, there are those who would like to think that there is freedom from risk in the status quo. However, humanity continues to be buffeted by ancient and new diseases, and by malnutrition and pollution; recombinant DNA techniques offer a reasonable expectation for a partial solution to some of these problems. Thus, we must ask whether we can afford to allow preoccupation with and conjecture about hazards that are not known to exist, to limit our ability to deal with hazards that do exist. Is there in fact greater risk in proceeding judiciously, or in not proceeding at all? We must ask whether there is any rational basis for predicting the dire consequences of recombinant DNA research portrayed in the scenarios proposed by some. We must then examine the "benefit" side of the picture and weigh the already realized benefits and the reasonable expectation of additional benefits, against the vague fear of the unknown that has in my opinion been the focal point of this controversy.

DNA ISSUES IN DISPUTE [4]

. . . During the assessment proceedings eight issues concerning the use of recombinant DNA technology have been raised, often fairly eloquently, and usually by nationally known scientists. Only one issue, however, has been addressed with any degree of seriousness. This selective attention deserves comment.

The questions raised have to do with safety, with political decision making, and with larger ethical issues.

Safety

1. The first area of controversy concerns what might be called operational safety issues. Microbiologists themselves raised the question of appropriate safety standards to be used in individual laboratories where work with pathological organisms would go forward. This issue has received prolonged and sustained attention from a wide segment of the scientific community; the issues involved have been sufficiently complex to preclude participation by many beyond the circle of scientific specialists, laboratory safety officers, and experts in statistical probability theory. But short-term safety issues *have* received considerable attention.

2. A second issue concerns longer-term laboratory safety questions that arise because of the proliferation of research. (How many experiments should go on at one time, and where, to minimize risks of accidents over time? Where will the cohorts of graduate students trained in the new techniques find jobs? How

[4] From chapter entitled "Why We Avoid the Key Questions: How Shifts in the Funding of Scientific Inquiry Affect Decision Making about Science," by Max Heirich, associate professor of sociology, University of Michigan. In *The Recombinant DNA Debate*. ed. by David A. Jackson and Stephen P. Stich. Prentice-Hall. '79. p 249-55. Copyright © 1979. Reprinted by permission of Prentice-Hall, Inc., Englewood Cliffs, N.J. 07632

will this affect the number of experiments occurring, the rate of application of findings, the ability to control application of safety standards? These questions view research activity, not from the standpoint of the individual laboratory, but as a *system* of activity that will generate its own accidents, misapplications, and problems over time, unless central coordination and planning is achieved early. This issue was raised, but never addressed directly.

3. A third safety issue has been all but ignored. How can the public be protected from unwise *applications* of new genetic principles? Some observers fear widespread environmental disruption could occur if the research is successful. Here are some examples of what they fear: new organisms developed to clean up oil spills might evade efforts to contain them, once the spills were under control. What would they do to other oil pools? Insulin-producing organisms that could produce cheap quantities of medicine also could wreak havoc if they escaped because they would send a normal population into insulin shock. Again, the ability to specify the sex of an unborn child, though a blessing to individual sets of parents, could seriously disrupt the ratio of men to women within a generation. They urge that the pace of discoveries be slowed down until the public can be protected from inappropriate application of such principles. Thus far, no assessment commission has seriously addressed this problem.

Political Decision Issues

A second series of issues has been raised with considerable rancor, frequently outside scientific and academic halls, although a few scientists also have been involved. Those who raise these issues recognize that the application of science regularly produces winners and losers—those who gain from the application and those who pay heavy costs. This political aspect of scientific inquiry—an embarrassment to the value-free intent of paradigm pursuit—has tended to be ignored within scientific discussions and among academics more generally. Thus it has been raised rather stridently, by representatives of interest groups who distrust the impact that current directions in scientific research are likely to have on their own self-interest.

4. One set of questions concerns appropriate locations for research laboratories. The Cambridge, Massachusetts, city council, for example, demanded assurance that its citizens would not be endangered by laboratory experiments at Harvard or MIT. And some scientists have urged that all work be conducted in a limited number of national laboratories.

5. Environmental lobbies and other citizen groups have demanded that "the public" and not simply the interests of researchers be represented in science policy decisions.

6. More radical groups ask why major funds should go toward additional research that could endanger the public instead of toward already-known solutions to public health problems. For example, why not remove carcinogenic agents in the natural environment, rather than discover ways to outwit their effects once they have entered the human body?

These questions have roused considerable heat. Few members of the intellectual community, however, have been willing to deal with the issues underlying them. For they threaten to take away the autonomy that scientists and intellectuals more generally have established for themselves. Many intellectuals see no substitute for self-regulation other than regulation through political means. They question the freedom of politicians to resist special-interest pressures, and so they fear the nature of any regulation that might occur.

Larger Ethical Issues

Beyond the question of who decides winners and losers from scientific inquiry, and how conflicts of interest are to be resolved, a more disturbing set of questions has been raised by a number of thoughtful scientists and scholars. They sound like contemporary reflections of two classic themes from literature, which might be described as the problem of the Sorcerer's Apprentice and the Faust dilemma.

7. Is it appropriate, some ask, to use nature's method for preserving species integrity to violate that integrity—just to see what will happen? At this stage of scientific discovery we do not know why species integrity exists as an organizing principle in nature or what the consequences of its violation are likely to be for the evolutionary process. The question is absolutely fundamental to the technology being used. It has been stated eloquently by some of the most respected scientists in the nation. Yet it has been totally ignored.

8. Others have asked whether we have any business exploring an area that will unlock major new power for human use before we show evidence that we have either the wisdom or else safeguarding mechanisms that will prevent disastrous misapplications of the principles. All participants agree that the research issues concern an area at least as important for application as was the development of atomic energy theory a generation ago, and fraught with equal potential for good use or bad. And all agree that the new technique is sufficiently simple and inexpensive to become available soon even to high school students. Yet intellectuals stand committed to the belief that the pursuit of knowledge is good and that the problems arising from its use remain someone else's specialty.

All of these questions seem basic and important. Yet only the first, which concerns safety standards for individual laboratories, has attracted serious and sustained attention. For this I think there are at least two reasons. First, it is the only question that does not challenge, at some level, the present arrangements for carrying on scientific inquiry. It is also more easily quantifiable and researchable than many of the other questions, but this is not sufficient reason to explain its selection for attention to the neglect of others.

The question about proliferation of laboratories and research personnel, for example, would seem a direct and logical extension of this question, yet scientists have moved vigorously to eliminate consideration of this issue as part of the safety question. (They have attempted to make them serial considerations, without acknowledging that decisions requested for the first issue could preclude solutions to the second part of the series.)

The question of winners and losers also seems amenable to assessment technologies common to science. But people have preferred to assume that there would be no losers, rather than to examine the question. Thus, while other issues *could* be pursued with some of the techniques currently at hand, these issues begin to challenge the arrangements by which the enterprise currently goes forward.

The issues concerning proliferation of research, for example, and concerning control of application of discoveries can be dealt with only if someone begins to assert control over the direction and pace of scientific inquiry. As we have seen, these issues threaten the autonomy now enjoyed by scientific communities, and they also would threaten the resource base that has become central to many universities across the nation. Small wonder that neither scientists nor the academic community more generally have been willing to devote sustained attention to these problems. They have been raised and discussed but then dismissed before anyone attempted the kind of careful assessment that has gone into questions of individual laboratory safety. This refusal to think about science from a systems perspective is extremely shortsighted: it will be very difficult to establish controls later after a certain research momentum has developed. But it seems clear that the scientific and academic communities are not prepared to face such issues directly.

The issues about who decides policy when interests are not in common, and what priorities should take precedence, are not welcomed by those who benefit most from the present decision arrangements. They have only been pursued outside the circles of scientists and academe.

The last two issues are perhaps the most fundamental and the most difficult to address. One could imagine that answers to the earlier questions might be formulated by national policymakers beyond the scientific community itself. Questions of rational system planning and of the involvement of relevant publics in the decision-making process are, after all, the kinds of questions that policymakers are accustomed to addressing. But the larger ethical questions, concerning appropriate strategy for scientific inquiry and the exploring of areas where findings could be misused, remain central to scientists themselves, rather than to other groups. They are much easier to evade than to face. Thus these questions have initially been overlooked, or dismissed with a brief argument, then resisted because addressing them would slow down the pace of research.

Many thoughtful critics have asked, why the hurry? The problem, as I see it, lies less with the race for eminence (for the Nobel prize, as some cynics have suggested) than with the dependence of individual scientists, and of the universities themselves, on federal moneys allocated with the expectation of rapid breakthroughs. To raise these questions not only puts individual careers in limbo, it also threatens the economic base upon which academia now depends. And in the absence of other mechanisms, it threatens to throw the scientific enterprise into the laps of vested political interests, because the questions strike so fundamentally at present arrangements for decision making in science.

Unresolved Issues in Science More Generally

The issues have been formulated above in terms of the immediate controversy concerning recombinant DNA research. Stated more generally, however, they extend to much larger areas of scientific inquiry. In question are socially desirable limits to the amount of scientific research, effective controls on the application of scientific findings that could damage population groups, the rights of various publics to take part in decisions that may affect their futures, and priorities for use of public funds: what kinds of questions deserve massive outlays of public funds, under what circumstances?

It should not surprise us that scientists do not find these questions attractive—for any answer to them is likely to challenge their present autonomy and privilege. So long as groups of scientists frame the questions that are addressed by policy-recommending groups, issues such as these are not likely to get sustained attention. Yet the recombinant DNA controversy makes it clear that the nature of scientific inquiry is changing. Questions such as these can be ignored only at real cost to all concerned, including the scientific community as well as the larger public.

The larger ethical issues also extend beyond the question of DNA research. They concern possible limits that scientists should impose *on themselves,* to avoid disruptive environmental consequences either from the pursuit of knowledge or from its application in new settings. They pose haunting questions that need answers from the collectivity of scientists. Because they challenge assumptions about progress through knowledge, assumptions that have guided scientific inquiry since its inception, they become especially difficult for intellectuals to pursue. Yet they cannot be ignored.

In the absence of alternative ways to make decisions, science finds itself in a dilemma. The present trend toward the merging of basic and applied science means that value issues no longer can be avoided; science begins to intervene too directly in the environment not to be considered a vested interest, to which others will respond. Yet, for the reasons just outlined, the scientific and intellectual communities are ill-equipped even to recognize, much less to respond effectively, to the more fundamental value issues being generated by their own work.

We need some new procedures for making decisions about science. We need them quickly, before it is too late to deal with some of the issues now being ignored. No new procedure will have much impact, however, unless it affects how funds are allocated for scientific research. As I see it, this would involve at least three changes in the way decisions now are made. First, some new device would have to be created for making decisions about the *pace* and *direction* of scientific inquiry. Second, some procedure would have to be developed for ensuring that an enlarged set of criteria are an explicit part of the decision process. Third, the range of parties involved in making such decisions would have to be expanded in a way that prevented the scientific community, the affluent special interests that would benefit from their work, or narrow political interests from defining the range of questions to be addressed. A social invention is called for, and soon. Who will make the first proposal?

BIBLIOGRAPHY

An asterisk (*) preceding a reference indicates that the article or part of it has been reprinted in this book.

BOOKS

Alsop, Stewart. Stay of execution: a sort of memoir. Lippincott. '73.

Augenstein, Leroy. Come, let us play God. Harper and Row. '76.

Barber, Bernard, and Lambert, R. D., eds. Medical ethics and social change. American Academy of Political and Social Science. new ed. '78.

Behnke, J. A. and Bok, Sissela, eds. The dilemmas of euthanasia. Anchor Press-Doubleday. '75.

Benton, R. G. Death and dying. Van Nostrand Reinhold. '78.

Brody, Baruch. Abortion and the sanctity of human life: a philosophical view. Massachusetts Institute of Technology Pr. '76.

Brody, Howard. Ethical decisions in medicine. Little, Brown. '76.

Brown, H. O. J. Death before birth. Nelson. '77.

Chavkin, Samuel. The mind stealers: psychosurgery and mind control. Houghton Mifflin. '78.

Connery, John. Abortion: the development of the Roman Catholic perspective. Loyola University Pr. '77.

DiGiacomo, James, ed. Abortion: a question of values. Winston Pr. '75.

Engelhardt, H. T. Jr. and Callahan, Daniel, eds. The foundations of ethics and its relationship to science. (Vol 1) Science, ethics and medicine. Institute of Society, Ethics and the Life Sciences, 360 Broadway, Hastings-on-Hudson, NY 10706. '76.

Finnis, John and others. The rights and wrongs of abortion. (Philosophy and Public Affairs Reader) Princeton University Pr. '74.

Fletcher, Joseph. Humanhood: essays in biomedical ethics. Prometheus Books, 1203 Kensington Avenue, Buffalo, NY 14215. '79.

Freund, P. A., ed. Experimentation with human subjects. Braziller. '70.

Gorovitz, Samuel and others, eds. Moral problems in medicine. Prentice-Hall. '76.

Hutton, Richard. Bio-revolution: DNA and the ethics of man-made life. New American Library. '78.

* Hyde, M. O. and Forsyth, E. H. Suicide: the hidden epidemic. Franklin Watts. '78.

211

Information Planning Associates. A bioethical perspective on death and dying. Information Planning Associates, Inc., 310 Maple Drive, Rockville, MD 20850. '77.

* Jackson, D. A. and Stich, S. P., eds. The recombinant DNA debate. Prentice-Hall. '79.

Koocher, G. P., ed. Children's rights and the mental health professions. (Personality Processes Series) Wiley. '76.

Kübler-Ross, Elisabeth. Death: the final stage of growth. Prentice-Hall. '75.

Kübler-Ross, Elisabeth. On death and dying. Macmillan. '69.

Kübler-Ross, Elisabeth. Questions and answers on death and dying. Macmillan. '74.

Kübler-Ross, Elisabeth. To live until we say goodbye. Prentice-Hall. '78.

Lear, John. Recombinant DNA. Crown. '78.

Leitenberg, Harold, ed. Handbook of behavior modification and behavior therapy. Prentice-Hall. '76.

Levinstein, J. L. and others. Biomedical ethics and Jewish law: a symposium sponsored by the Mount Sinai Hospital Medical Center Board of Trustees, October 24. '76. Mount Sinai Hospital Medical Center, Chicago, IL. '76.

* Lygre, D. G. Life manipulation: from test-tube babies to aging. Walker. '79.

Maguire, D. C. Death by choice. Doubleday. '74.

Mappes, T. A. and Zembaty, J. S., eds. Social ethics: morality and social policy. McGraw-Hill. '77.

Mechanic, David. The growth of bureaucratic medicine: an inquiry into the dynamics of patient behavior and the organization of medical care. (Health, Medicine and Society Series) Wiley. '76.

Mertens, T. R., comp. Human genetics: readings on the implications of genetic engineering. Wiley. '75.

Mohr, J. C. Abortion in America: the origins and evolution of national policy. Oxford University Pr. '78.

Noonan, J. T. Jr. Private choice: abortion in America in the seventies. Free Pr. '79.

Oden, T. C. Should treatment be terminated? Harper and Row. '76.

Quinlan, Joseph and Quinlan, Julia. Karen Ann: the Quinlans tell their story. Doubleday. '77.

Reed, Evelyn and Moriarty, Claire. Abortion and the Catholic church: two feminists defend women's rights. Pathfinder Pr. '73.

Reiser, S. J., Dyck, A. J., and Curran, W. J., eds. Ethics in medicine: historical perspectives and contemporary concerns. Massachusetts Institute of Technology Pr. '77.

Restak, R. M. Premeditated man: bioethics and the control of future human life. Penguin Books. '77.

Ribes, Bruno. Biology and ethics. United Nations Educational, Scientific and Cultural Organizations. Unipub. '78.

Rifkin, Jeremy, and Howard, Ted. Who should play God?: the artificial creation of life and what it means for the future of the human race. Delacorte. '77.

Russell, O. R. Freedom to die: moral and legal aspects of euthanasia. Human Sciences Pr. revised ed '77.

Sass, L. R., ed. Abortion: freedom of choice and the right to life. Facts on File. '78.

Shannon, T. A., ed. Bioethics: basic writings on the key ethical questions that surround the major, modern biological possibilities and problems. Paulist Pr. '76.

Stein, J. J. Making medical choices: ethics and medicine in a technological age. Houghton Mifflin. '78.

Tobach, Ethel, and Proshansky, H. M., eds. Genetic destiny: race as a scientific and social controversy. AMS Pr. '76.

Veatch, R. M. Case studies in medical ethics. Harvard University Pr. '77.

Veatch, R. M. Death, dying and the biological revolution: our last quest for responsibility. Yale University. '76.

Wade, Nicholas. The ultimate experiment: man-made evolution. Walker. '77.

Wertenbaker, L. T. Death of a man. Beacon Pr. '74.

Wojcik, Jan. Muted consent: a casebook in modern medical ethics. West Lafayette, Ind. Purdue University. '78.

Woods, John. Engineered death: abortion, suicide, euthanasia and senecide. University of Ottawa Pr. '78.

PERIODICALS

American Biology Teacher. 41:176-80. Mr. '79. Can bioethics be taught? G. H. Kieffer.

Atlantic. 239:43-62. F. '77. Science that frightens scientists: the great debate over DNA. William Bennett and Joel Gurin.

BioScience. 25:608+. O. '76. Gazing into the crystal ball; recombinant DNA research. Ruth Hubbard.

BioScience. 26:609-10. O. '76. Freedom of inquiry and scientific responsibility; recombinant DNA research. R. B. Helling and S. L. Allen.

BioScience. 27:277-8. Ap. '77. The scientist: trustee for humanity. Bentley Glass.

BioScience. 27:317-9. My. '77. Recombinant DNA forum—stellar cast; gripping plot; but no new message. E. M. Leeper.

BioScience. 28:392-3. Je. '78. On animal and human sociobiology. Adam Lomnicki.

BioScience. 28:718-21. N. '78. Brotherhood and lifeboat ethics. J. D. Martin.

Boston Sunday Globe: New England magazine. p 24-9. Jl. 9, '78. Closing in on cloning. Larry Stains.

Bulletin of the Atomic Scientists. 33:4-5. O. '77. Recombinant DNA technology: who shall regulate? Susan Wright.

Christianity Today. 23:32-3. Ap. 6, '79. What is human life anyway? J. R. W. Stott.

Commonweal. 102:585-9. D. 5, '75. Death on demand. P. F. and C. A. Berger.

* Commonweal. 102:589-90. D. 5, '75. A triumph of technology. T. A. Shannon.

Commonweal. 103:232-3+. Ap. 9, '76. Death comes to life. Peter Steinfels.

* Commonweal. 105:547-8. S. 1, '78. Test-tube babies.

Commonweal. 105:771-3. D. 8, '78. Do Catholics have constitutional rights? Hyde Amendment challenge.

Commonweal. 106:394-7. Jl. 6, '79. Redefining death. W. G. Jeffko.

Editorial Research Reports. v 2, no 15:767-84. O. 22, '76. Abortion politics. Sandra Stencel.

Editorial Research Reports. v 2, no 15:767-84. O. 22, '76. Abortion politics. Sandra Stencel.

* Editorial Research Reports. v 1, no 12:225-44. Mr. 25, '77. Genetic research. Sandra Stencel.

* Editorial Research Reports. v 1, no 4:63-80. Ja. 27, '78. Right to death. H. B. Shaffer.

Environment. 19:31-7. Ap. '77. Research in a box: recombinant DNA research. Julian McCaull.

Family Health. 10:39+. S. '78. Euthanasia: the deadly dilemma.

Family Health. 10:22-4. D. '78. New arrival: the test-tube baby. Interview edited by J. N. Egan. W. J. Sweeney III.

Family Health. 11:28-31. My. '79. Genetic engineering: where will it lead? Edward Edelson.

Fortune. 97:100-4+. Je. 19, '78. The cloning era is almost here. Gene Bylinsky.

* Futurist. 12:331-2. O. '78. Surviving the new biology. Review of Bio-Babel: Can We Survive the New Biology? by A. R. Utke. John Knox Press. Atlanta. '78.

* Harper's. 257:21-9. Ag. '78. Bioethical questions. L. C. Lewin.

Holton, Gerald and Robert S. Morison, eds. Limits of scientific inquiry. Norton. '79.

* Human Behavior. 7:58. Mr. '78. Changing views of abortion; study by Theodore Wagenaar and Ingeborg W. Knol.

Nathanson, Bernard M. and Richard Ostling. Aborting America. Doubleday. '79.

* New York Sunday News Magazine. p. 13-14+. D. 31, '78. The living will. Harry Bernstein.

New York Times. p E17. Ag. 6, '78. Life in the test tube. R. A. McCormick.

New York Times. p A16. Mr. 6, '79. The religious case for abortion rights. Soma Golden.

New York Times. p A18. Mr. 9, '79. Artificial insemination of single women poses difficult questions. Georgia Dullea.

New York Times Magazine. p 70-80. Ap. 17, '77. Between guilt and gratification: abortion doctors reveal their feelings. Norma Rosen.

New York Times Magazine. p 30-33. Ja. 14, '79. Catching them before suicide. Jim Jerome.

Newsweek. 91:68-9. Mr. 20, '78. All about clones. Peter Gwynne and others.

Newsweek. 92:76. Jl. 24, '78. The test-tube baby; case of L. Brown. Peter Gwynne.

Newsweek. 92:66-72. Ag. 7, '78. All about that baby. Peter Gwynne and others.

Newsweek. 94:87. Jl. 2, '79. Rational suicide? case of J. Roman. D. K. Shah and Mariana Gosnell.

* Philosophy & Public Affairs. 8:88-99. Fall '78. An alternative policy for obtaining cadaver organs for transplantation. J. L. Muyskens.

* Psychology Today. 11:20-3. N. '77. Experiments on humans: where to draw the line? Perry London.

Psychology Today. 11:23-4. My. '78. Is sociobiology all wet? Maya Pines.

Psychology Today. 12:122. O. '78. Is there a right way to die? Norman Klein.

* RN. 41:74-6+. D. '78. Are you too sure of your stand on the right to die? M. S. Gates and G. G. Mayer.

Saturday Review. 3:55. S. 18, '76. Danger: biologists at work; recombinant DNA rules. Anthony Wolff.

Saturday Review. 5:14-20. D. 10, '77. When man becomes as God: the biological prospect. Albert Rosenfeld.

* Saturday Review. 5:10-14. O. 28, '78. The case for test-tube babies. Albert Rosenfeld.

* Science. 190:1271-5. D. 26, '75. The Haemmerli affair: is passive euthanasia murder? B. J. Culliton.

Science. 192:236-8. Ap. 16, '76. Recombinant DNA: the last look before the leap. Nicholas Wade.

Science. 193:215-7. Jl. 16, '76. Recombinant DNA: chimeras set free under guard. Nicholas Wade.

* Science. 193:1105-6. S. 17, '76. Helping the dying die: two Harvard hospitals go public with policies. B. J. Culliton.

Science. 194:299-301. O. 15, '76. Psychosurgery: national commission issues surprisingly favorable report. B. J. Culliton.

Science. 194:303-6. O. 15, '76. Recombinant DNA: a critic questions the right to free inquiry. Nicholas Wade.

Science. 194:1133-5. D. 10, '76. Recombinant DNA research: beyond the NIH guidelines. Clifford Grobstein.

* Science. 195:654-7. F. 18, '77. Recombinant DNA: fact and fiction. S. N. Cohen.

Science. 196:127. Ap. 8, '77. The recombinant DNA debate. M. F. Singer.

Science. 196:159-60. Ap. 8, '77. Recombinant DNA: examples of present-day research. John Abelson.

Science. 198:677-8. N. 18, '77. Old problems, new challenges. Valerie Miké and R. A. Good.

Science. 198:690-3. N. 18, '77. Acquiring new information while retaining old ethics. Victor Herbert.

Science. 198:699-705. N. 18, '77. The code of the scientist and its relationship to ethics; address, May 27, '77. André Cournand.

Science. 198:1105-10. D. 16, '77. Social imperatives of medical research. Leon Eisenberg.

Science. 199:1314-16. Mr. 24, '78. Scientists dispute book's claim that human clone has been born. B. J. Culliton.

Science. 201:698-9. Ag. 25, '78. In vitro fertilization: is it safe and repeatable? Interviews ed. by Gina Bari Kolata. J. D. Schulman, F. Fuchs.

Science. 201:1094-1101. S. 22, '78. Research involving human subjects. B. H. Gray and others.

Science. 202:198-9. O. 13, '78. Ethics advisory board confronts conception in the test tube. B. J. Culliton.

Science. 205:171. Jl. 13, '79. Test tube fertilization research seen acceptable; Ethics Advisory Board report. John Walsh.

Science Digest. 81:21-2. Je. '77. Recombinant DNA debate shakes science community. D. W. McMullen.

Science Digest. 82:62-5+. Jl. '77. DNA: will the future curse science's decisions today? Marc Reisner.

Science Digest. 84:7-12. O. '78. A happy accident? More test-tube babies? Peter Gwynne

Science Digest. 84:24. D. '78. DNA milestone: dawn of an age?

Science News. 109:231. Ap. 10, '76. Genetic engineering: a mammalian first.

Science News. 109:389. Je. 19, '76. Recombinant DNA: impacts and advances.

Science News. 111:181. Mr. 19, '77. Recombinant DNA: clashing views aired.

Science News. 111:216-7. Ap. 2, '77. Recombinant DNA research. J. A. Miller.

Science News. 111:314-5+. My. 14, '77. Psychosurgery at the crossroads. Joel Greenberg.

Science News. 113:164. Mr. 18, '78. Cloning of a man: debate begins.

Science News. 114:84. Ag. 5, '78. Louise: birth of a new technology.

Science News. 114:407. D. 9, '78. U.S. gears up for test-tube babies.

Sciences, The. 19:22-4. Ja. '79. Give me liberty. Gerald Weissmann.

Scientific American. 236:21-7. Ja. '77. Legal abortion. Christopher Tietze and Sarah Lewit.

Scientific American. 237:22-33. Jl. '77. Recombinant-DNA debate. Clifford Grobstein.

Smithsonian. 9:50-7. N. '78. Modern bioengineers reinvent human anatomy with spare parts. Maya Pines.

Time. 108:101. O. 11, '76. The right to die; California law.

Time. 109:32-45. Ap. 18, '77. Tinkering with life.

* Time. 110:49. Ag. 1, '77. Of abortion and the unfairness of life. Lance Morrow.

Time. 110:56. Ag. 15, '77. DNA research: not so dangerous after all?

Time. 112:58-9. Jl. 31, '78. The first test-tube baby; case of L. Brown.

* Time. 112:69. Jl. 31, '78. To fool (or not) with mother nature.

Time. 112:68. Ag. 7, '78. Test-tube baby: it's a girl; case of L. Brown.

* Time. 114:26-7. Jl. 9, '79. The fanatical abortion fight.

USA Today. 107:14. D. '78. Needed: euthanasia criteria.

* U.S. News & World Report. 82:80-1. Ap. 11, '77. Creating new forms of life—blessing or curse?

U.S. News & World Report. 85:24. Jl. 31, '78. England's test-tube baby.

U.S. News & World Report. 85:22-3. Ag. 7, '78. Rush of test-tube babies ahead?

* U.S. News & World Report. 85:67-70. N. 13, '78. Death in America: no longer a hidden subject. S. N. Wellborn.

Washington Post. p A3. Jl. 28, '78. Theologians react cautiously to test-tube baby process. Marjorie Hyer.

Washington Post. p B7. Jl. 30, '78. Irreverent test tubes. G. F. Will.